True Tales™
from the
Mountains

Henry Billings

Melissa Stone Billings

STECK-VAUGHN
COMPANY

A Division of Harcourt Brace & Company

www.steck-vaughn.com

Acknowledgments

Executive Editor: Stephanie Muller
Senior Editor: Kristy Schulz
Project Editor: Meredith Edgley O'Reilly
Associate Director of Design: Cynthia Ellis
Design Manager: Alexandra Corona
Media Researcher: Claudette Landry
Electronic Production Artist: Dina Instinski
Electronic Production Specialist: Alan Klemp

Cartography: MapQuest.com, Inc.
Illustration Credits: P.108b Kathie Kelleher
Photo Credits: Cover (inset) ©Jeff Schultz/AlaskaStock Images; Cover (rope) Rick Williams; Cover (background, compass), p.1 ©PhotoDisc; p.3 ©PhotoDisc; p.6 David Muench/Corbis; p.8 ©North Wind Pictures; p.9 Corbis-Bettmann; p.10 ©North Wind Pictures; p.14 (portrait) Denver Public Library, Western History Collection; p.14 (frame) Plumas County Museum; p.14 (background) ©Superstock; p.16 Joslyn Art Museum, Omaha, Nebraska, Gift of Enron Art Foundation; pp.17–18 Plumas County Museum; p.22 Brown Brothers; p.24 The Granger Collection; p.25 ©Superstock; p.26 Brown Brothers; p.30 Superstock; pp.32, 33 The Everett Collection; p.34 Galen Rowell/Corbis; p.38 ©Superstock; pp.40, 41 Ted Streshinsky/Corbis; p.42 Department of Special Collections, University Research Library, UCLA Collection 1429, Los Angeles Times, Box 774. Neg. #282977 Portrait of Lauren Elder 4/29/76; pp.46, 48, 49, 50 ©Arlene Blum; p.54 ©Scott Spiker/AlaskaStock Images; p.56 ©Superstock; pp.57, 58 ©Scott Takushi/Seattle Times; p.62 ©Lanl/Sygma; p.64 Jeremy Horner/Corbis; p.65 ©Jeff Topping/NYT Pictures; p.66 Roger Ressmeyer/©Corbis; p.70 ©Todd Huston; p.72 ©Hugh Rose/AlaskaStock Images; pp.73, 74 ©Todd Huston; p.78 ©Gamma Liaison; p.80t CORBIS/George Hall; p.80b ©Juan Manuel Renjifo/Earth Scenes; p.81 Fernando Llano/AP/Wide World; p.82 AP/Wide World; p.86 ©Scott Fischer/Woodfin Camp; p.88 ©Neal Beidelman/Woodfin Camp; pp.89–90 ©Scott Fischer/Woodfin Camp; p.94 ©Jeff Schultz/AlaskaStock Images; p.96t Marc Muench/Corbis; p.96b The Olympian, Craig Sailor/AP/Wide World; p.97 The News Tribune, Duncan Livingston/AP Wide World; p.98 The Olympian, Craig Sailor/AP/Wide World; p.108t ©PhotoDisc; p.108m www.corbis.com/Pat O'Hara; p.109t www.corbis.com/Galen Rowell; p.109m www.corbis.com/Craig Lovell; p.109b (both) WP Wergin, ARS-USDA.

Contents

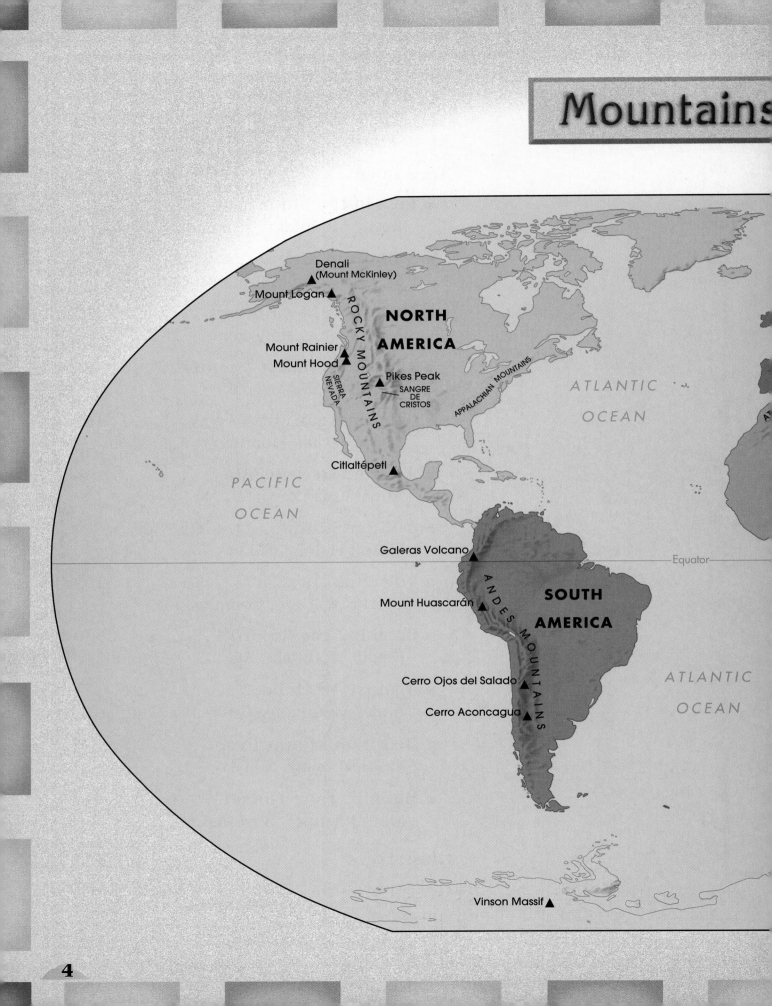

Denali
(Mount McKinley) ▲

Mount Logan ▲

ROCKY MOUNTAINS

**NORTH
AMERICA**

Mount Rainier ▲

Mount Hood ▲

SIERRA
NEVADA

Pikes Peak ▲

SANGRE
DE
CRISTOS

APPALACHIAN MOUNTAINS

ATLANTIC

OCEAN

Citlaltépetl ▲

PACIFIC

OCEAN

Galeras Volcano ▲

Equator

Mount Huascarán ▲

ANDES MOUNTAINS

**SOUTH
AMERICA**

ATLANTIC

OCEAN

Cerro Ojos del Salado ▲

Cerro Aconcagua ▲

Vinson Massif ▲

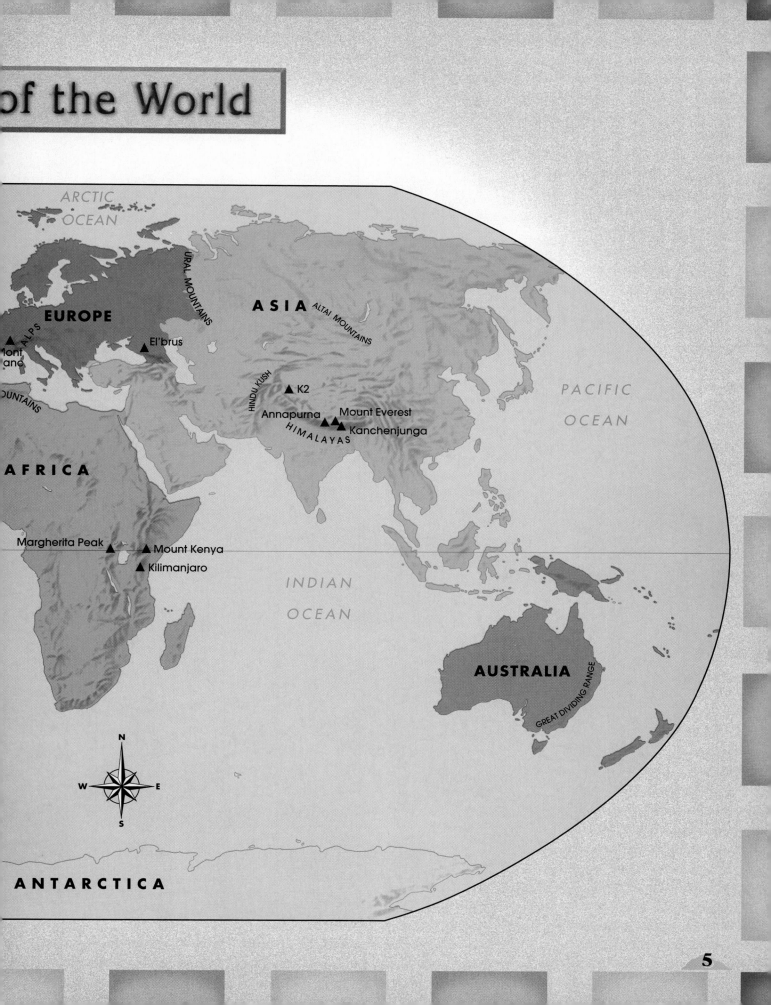

ARCTIC
OCEAN

EUROPE

ASIA

URAL MOUNTAINS

ALTAI MOUNTAINS

ALPS

El'brus

Mont
Blanc

MOUNTAINS

HINDU KUSH

▲ K2

Annapurna ▲▲ Mount Everest

HIMALAYAS ▲ Kanchenjunga

PACIFIC
OCEAN

AFRICA

Margherita Peak ▲ ▲ Mount Kenya

▲ Kilimanjaro

INDIAN

OCEAN

AUSTRALIA

GREAT DIVIDING RANGE

N

W   E

S

ANTARCTICA

Lost in the Mountains

Zebulon Pike stared at the huge mountains rising up in the distance. He could see that the **peaks** were covered in snow. It would be hard to reach the mountains and even harder to cross them. But still the men went on. They did not know that they were on a journey that would almost cost them their lives.

Pike's Mistake

Zebulon Pike was an American soldier. In 1806 the United States Army sent him to the area of land that is now central Colorado. The Army wanted Pike to find the **sources** of the Arkansas and Red rivers. The Army also wanted Pike to take several Osage Indians to their village. Twenty-one men, including 19 soldiers, went with Pike and the Osage.

The group headed out in July. Pike's men took the Osage to their village and then continued the journey. In October, six soldiers left to create maps of the area. By November, the remaining 16 men were nearing the Rocky Mountains. Winter was approaching. The men were not dressed for a winter in the mountains. They wore thin clothes. Few of the men had socks, and even fewer had hats. Still, Pike ordered his men to go on.

When Pike caught sight of the great mountain in November, he knew he shouldn't take the time to climb it. But he thought he could reach the **summit** in one day. The view would help him learn more about the area. Pike and three men walked all day but didn't even get to the base of the 14,110-foot

Zebulon Pike

mountain. The air was cold, and the snow was deep. By the second day, the men were hungry, cold, and growing weak.

After the third day, Pike admitted that he had made a mistake. The mountain was still miles away. Pike wrote in his journal that it would have taken another day's march just to reach the mountain's base. Besides, Pike believed that no person could **ascend** to the top of the steep mountain. So, Pike turned around without ever reaching the mountain. But the mountain is known today as Pikes Peak, because Pike sighted it.

Lost in the Cold

Pike hurried the 15 soldiers along the Arkansas River. The days were getting shorter and colder. It snowed often. At night, the men had to sleep on the wet ground. They had no blankets because they had cut them up to use as socks. They **survived** by building huge fires and staying near the flames.

Pike tried to follow the Arkansas River to its source, but again and again the river divided. Pike never knew which **fork** to take. In time, the group became lost. At one point, they thought they had found the Red River, so they followed it instead. But the river was frozen, and their horses often fell on the ice.

After several days of this, the men came to a **landmark** they recognized. Suddenly, the truth was clear. They were not on the Red River at all. They were back on the Arkansas River.

At that point, Pike could have followed the Arkansas River back to **civilization**. But he wanted to find the Red River. So Pike and his men headed toward a tall **mountain range** known as the Sangre de Cristos. The peaks of these mountains were covered with snow. To cross them would not be easy.

The horses were too lame to make the trip, so Pike ordered two of his men to stay behind and care for them. Promising to send someone back for the men later, Pike and the others set out on foot.

A Miserable March

On January 14, 1807, Pike's group came to a valley near the base of the Sangre de Cristos. Unfortunately, they arrived just as a **blizzard** began. There was no shelter from the snowy storm. There wasn't even enough wood to make a fire.

By evening, nine men had frozen feet. The five men who could still walk had no luck gathering food. So they waited, cold and miserable, for the storm to end. Days passed. When at last Pike killed a buffalo, it was the first food the men had eaten in four days.

On January 22, Pike tried to get the group moving again. But two of the men, John Sparks and Thomas Dougherty, still couldn't walk. Pike knew he would have to leave them behind. Leaving them with rifles and meat, he told Sparks and Dougherty to be brave. Pike then promised that someone would return for them soon.

Pike and his men had no shelter from the cold blizzard.

Pike now had only eleven men marching with him. As the group struggled on through the mountains, the snow was deeper than ever. Often, the men had to push through snow up to their waist. They couldn't find food. Soon another soldier, Hugh Menaugh, became too weak to travel. He was left behind, too.

Finally, Pike's group crossed the Sangre de Cristos. Pike wrote that they could not have survived one more day in the mountains. The men quickly built a shelter.

On February 7, Pike sent men back to get Menaugh, Dougherty, and Sparks. Menaugh was brought back, but Dougherty and Sparks could not travel. Their frozen feet had turned black and mushy. They pulled bones from their rotted toes and asked the group to take these to Pike. It was their way of asking him to save them. Pike quickly sent another group out to get them. He also arranged to get the two men and the horses left back at the Arkansas River.

Zebulon Pike never did find the Red River. He also never found the source of the Arkansas River. But he survived a winter in the Colorado mountains and brought all his men back alive. He also gave his name to a world-famous mountain, Pikes Peak.

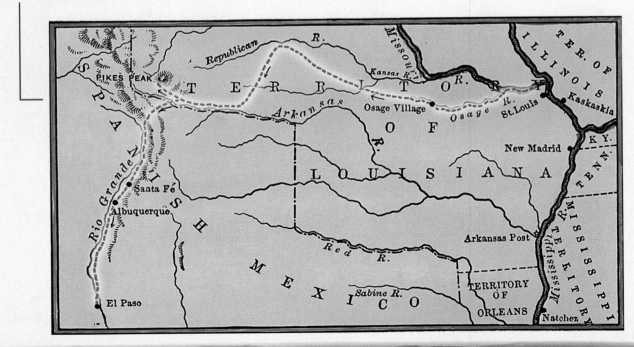

Pike traveled west to find the source of the Arkansas River.

USE WHAT YOU KNOW

Read and Remember — Finish the Sentence

▲ **Circle the best ending for each sentence.**

1. Zebulon Pike was an American _____.
President   farmer   soldier

2. Pike and his men neared the Rocky Mountains in _____.
1906   1806   1850

3. Pike and his men suffered from _____.
the heat   the cold   lack of water

4. The tall mountain that Pike saw was later named _____.
Osage   Pikes Peak   the Arkansas

5. The men headed to the Sangre de Cristos Mountains _____.
on foot   in summer   with plenty of food

Think About It — Drawing Conclusions

▲ **Write one or more sentences to answer each question.**

1. Why was it dangerous that Pike's men were dressed in thin clothes?

_____

2. Why, do you think, did Pike bring horses on the trip?_____

_____

3. Why did Pike's group have trouble finding food in the Sangre de

Cristos Mountains?_____

_____

4. Why did Pike have to leave Dougherty and Sparks behind?_____

_____

Focus on Vocabulary — Find the Meaning

▲ **Read each sentence. Circle the best meaning for the word in dark print.**

1. Zebulon Pike could see that the **peaks** were covered in snow.

   long boards   mountain tops   trees

2. Pike and his men tried to find the **sources** of the two rivers.

   starting points   real names   owners

3. Pike thought he could reach the **summit** in one day.

   store   top   warm weather

4. Pike believed that no person could **ascend** to the top of the mountain.

   see   be carried   climb up

5. The men **survived** by building huge fires.

   had fun   found food   stayed alive

6. Pike never knew which **fork** to take.

   place where a river divides   camp   pair of boots

7. The men came to a **landmark** they recognized.

   stream   familiar object   town

8. Pike could have followed the river back to **civilization**.

   a cave   cities and towns   a waterfall

9. The men headed toward a tall **mountain range**.

   group of mountains   stranger   hill

10. The men arrived at the Sangre de Cristos Mountains just as a **blizzard** began.

    war   bad snowstorm   new season

Continents and Oceans

Zebulon Pike explored the Rocky Mountains on the **continent** of North America. A continent is a large body of land. Earth also has large bodies of water called oceans. Look at the map of the world below. Write the answer to each question.

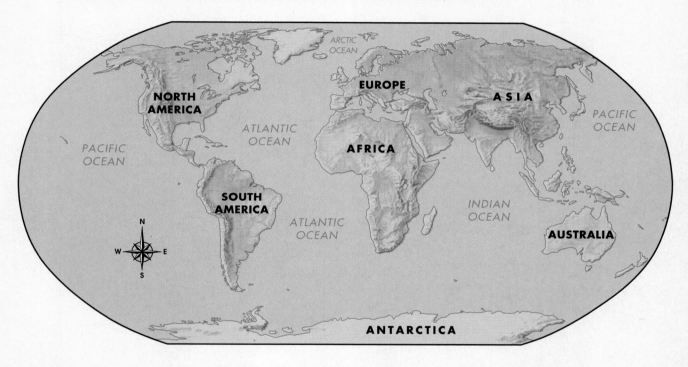

1. How many continents are there? _____

2. What are the names of the continents? _____

_____

3. Which two continents do not touch any other continents? _____

_____

4. Which ocean separates Africa and Australia? _____

5. Which ocean is along both South America and Asia? _____

6. Which five continents are along the Atlantic Ocean? _____

_____

Mountain Man

J im Beckwourth couldn't wait to get out of St. Louis, Missouri. He didn't like the job that he had in a **blacksmith** shop. Beckwourth had heard that life in the West was more exciting. People there could explore the wilderness and live off the land. So in 1823, at the age of 23, Jim Beckwourth headed west to the **frontier**.

Making a Promise

Beckwourth, an African American, joined a fur company heading to the Rocky Mountains. To get there, the group had to cross large **plains**, or flat land. However, they left late in the year and were hit by one blizzard after another. Soon their food supply ran out. The men were in danger of starving to death. Their leader asked the best hunters in the group to try to find food. Beckwourth grabbed his rifle and set out.

Beckwourth managed to kill a duck. But he was so hungry that he sat down and ate the entire thing himself. As soon as he had finished, he felt ashamed of himself. He thought of the men back at camp. He knew they were just as cold, weak, and hungry as he was. Beckwourth made himself a promise. From then on, he would never refuse to share his last bite of food, his last bit of money, or his only blanket with a friend.

Luckily, Beckwourth found and shot a deer and three elk. So he returned to camp with plenty of food for everyone. But Jim Beckwourth never forgot the

The Crow Indians were friends with James Beckwourth.

promise he had made after eating that duck. It was a promise that he kept for the rest of his life.

When the group finally reached the Rockies, Beckwourth went off on his own. He made friends with Crow Indians and went to live with them. He even became a Crow war chief. But after ten years, Beckwourth left the Crow village to travel again.

During his many years as a mountain man, Beckwourth lived through all kinds of weather. He traveled across the roughest **terrain**. He later wrote that he crossed the Rocky Mountains "in summer heats and winter frosts." For food, he hunted, fished, and trapped. For clothes, he wore animal furs. There were times when he was sick or when he couldn't find food. Still, he was happy. He loved the freedom and the beauty of the mountains.

The Sierra Nevada Mountains

In 1848 Beckwourth left the Rocky Mountains and went further west. Gold was soon discovered in California. Like many others, Beckwourth hoped to find his fortune in gold. To get to California, he had to cross the Sierra Nevada Mountains.

This was not a problem for Beckwourth. But it was a problem for most settlers in wagons. The peaks of the Sierra Nevada Mountains were steep, and the

canyons were deep. It was almost impossible to get wagons across the mountains. Most settlers left their wagons behind and struggled across on foot. Sometimes they would get lost. Many settlers starved to death.

Traveling along a high trail in 1850, Beckwourth saw an area of the mountains that seemed to be lower than other parts. Later, Beckwourth and some friends returned to the area. All the others "busied themselves in searching for gold...," said Beckwourth, "but... I had come to discover what I suspected to be a **pass**."

Jim Beckwourth was right. It was a pass. In fact, it was a much easier way through the Sierra Nevada Mountains than any other trail in the area.

Beckwourth's Pass

Beckwourth hurried to Marysville, California. He told the people there about his discovery. The new pass would lead settlers right to Marysville, bringing a lot of new business. So the town agreed to help pay for the cost of turning the pass into a road.

Beckwourth worked hard on the road. He spent $1,600 of his own money to build it. Then, when he was almost finished, he became very ill. An **infection** raged through his body. Beckwourth gave up all hope

Beckwourth's Pass was a low area in the Sierra Nevada Mountains.

Settlers often stopped at James Beckwourth's trading post.

of getting out of the mountains alive. The nearest doctor was over a hundred miles away.

Luckily, a **wagon train** happened by. The women in the group nursed Beckwourth back to health. When he was strong enough, he offered to lead the 17 wagons to Marysville. They agreed. Beckwourth soon led the first wagon train through Beckwourth's Pass.

As Beckwourth expected, the pass became very popular. Thousands of settlers used it. But a fire burned down much of Marysville, so the town could not afford to pay Beckwourth his money.

Beckwourth was disappointed. But he built a house and **trading post** near the entrance to Beckwourth's Pass. Often, settlers stumbled to his door, **desperate** for food and shelter. In most cases, they had no money at all. Beckwourth remembered the promise that he had made to share whatever he had. "They never were refused what they asked for at my house," he wrote.

In 1856 Beckwourth wrote a book about his life. He called it *The Life and Adventures of James P. Beckwourth*. Ten years later, during a visit to the Crow Indians, his old friends, Jim Beckwourth died. He was buried there, among the mountains he loved so much.

USE WHAT YOU KNOW

Read and Remember — Check the Events

Place a check in front of the three sentences that tell what happened in the story.

_____ **1.** Jim Beckwourth spent many years living near the ocean.

_____ **2.** The Crow Indians became friends with Jim Beckwourth.

_____ **3.** Jim Beckwourth found a new way to get through the Sierra Nevada Mountains.

_____ **4.** Many settlers became trapped in Beckwourth's Pass.

_____ **5.** Jim Beckwourth wrote a book about his years in the mountains.

_____ **6.** The town of Marysville asked Jim Beckwourth to help fight the Crow Indians.

Write About It

Imagine you were a newspaper reporter in the 1800s. You are about to interview Jim Beckwourth. Write three questions that you would like to ask him.

1. _____

_____

2. _____

_____

3. _____

_____

Focus on Vocabulary — Make a Word

Choose a word in dark print to complete each sentence. Write the letters of the word on the blanks. When you are finished, the letters in the circles will tell where Beckwourth's Pass led.

blacksmith	**plains**	**canyons**	**infection**
trading post	**frontier**	**terrain**	**pass**
wagon train	**desperate**		

1. The Sierra Nevada Mountains have some deep _____.

   ◯ _ _ _ _ _ _ _

2. Beckwourth discovered a low _____ through the mountains.

   ◯ _ _ _ _

3. People crossed the flat _____ to get to the Rocky Mountains.

   ◯ _ _ _ _ _ _

4. Many people bought supplies at the _____ Beckwourth built.

   _ _ _ _ _ _ _ ◯ _ _ _ _

5. Beckwourth liked life on the _____, away from cities.

   ◯ _ _ _ _ _ _ _

6. Beckwourth led the first _____ through his pass.

   _ _ _ _ _ ◯ _ _ _ _ _

7. Beckwourth fed starving people who were _____ for food.

   _ _ _ _ ◯ _ _ _ _

8. Beckwourth became sick with an _____.

   ◯ _ _ _ _ _ _ _ _

9. Mountain men traveled across rough land, or _____.

   _ _ _ ◯ _ _ _

10. Beckwourth once worked in a _____ shop.

   ◯ _ _ _ _ _ _ _ _

USE A MAP

Map Directions

The four main directions are **north**, **south**, **east**, and **west**. On maps they are shown on a **compass rose**. In-between directions are **northeast**, **southeast**, **southwest**, and **northwest**. The map below shows some places James Beckwourth visited during his life. Study the map. Circle the answer that best completes each sentence below.

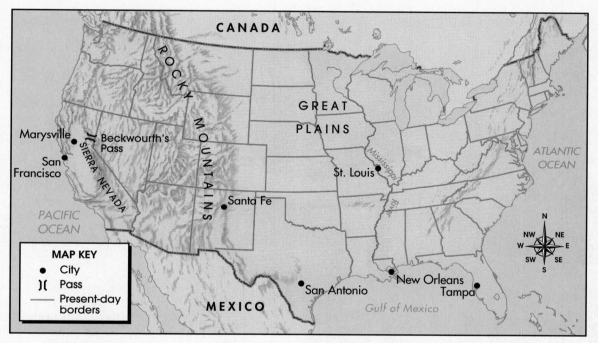

1. St. Louis is _____ of the Rocky Mountains.

    north   east   southwest

2. San Antonio is west of _____.

    Tampa   Santa Fe   Marysville

3. San Francisco is _____ of Beckwourth's Pass.

    southwest   northeast   north

4. To get from Santa Fe to Beckwourth's Pass, travel _____.

    southwest   northwest   east

Queen of the Climbers

The people of Peru's town of Yungay sighed, "Poor Miss Peck." They didn't think she could make it to the top. Even Annie Smith Peck herself had some doubts. Peck had already tried five times to climb Mount Huascarán, the highest peak in Peru. Each effort had ended in **failure**. Now, on August 28, 1908, she was getting ready to try again. If she made it, Peck would be the first person ever to reach the peak.

A Love of Mountains

Annie Smith Peck began thinking about mountain climbing when she was 35 years old. That was when this American professor saw the Alps in Switzerland. The beauty of these mountains amazed her. When she saw the Matterhorn, a 14,690-foot mountain of the Alps, she knew that she wanted to climb it some day.

Peck began slowly. First, she climbed small mountains in Greece and Switzerland. Then she climbed California's Mount Shasta, which has an **altitude** of 14,162 feet. But Peck wanted to climb even higher. In 1895 she became the third woman to climb the Matterhorn. This made her famous.

By then, Peck had quit her job as a college professor. She **supported** herself by giving talks about mountain climbing. Peck became known as the "Queen of the Climbers." She climbed as often as she could.

When she was 45, Peck decided that she wanted to climb a mountain no one had ever climbed. She practiced by climbing two peaks in Mexico and other peaks in Europe. Then she decided to head to Mount Sorata in Bolivia, a country in South America. No one had ever **conquered** Mount Sorata. It took Peck four years to raise enough money for the climbing trip.

In 1903 Peck finally began her attempt to climb Mount Sorata. She failed. The next year she tried once more, but again she didn't make it. She missed reaching the 20,867-foot peak by just 367 feet!

It wasn't really Peck's fault. The guides and **porters** she had hired were not loyal and were sometimes lazy. They did not know as much about mountain climbing as they said they did. In fact, while Peck was crossing an ice bridge, the guides even refused to hold a safety rope attached to her. One false step would have caused her to **plunge** hundreds of feet to her death.

Climbing in Peru

After her second failure, Peck gave up on Mount Sorata. Instead, she decided to try an even higher mountain in Peru. Mount Huascarán, part of the Andes mountain chain, had never been climbed before. Even though it is close to the **equator**, it is a very dangerous and icy mountain. Even Peck was shocked by its enormous snow fields and deadly **crevasses**. Peck later wrote that when she first saw Mount Huascarán, she "was filled with **dismay**."

But Peck was determined to climb the mountain. She began with some of the same problems that she had when she climbed Mount Sorata. She had to spend months raising the necessary cash. She also had trouble hiring loyal, helpful people.

The people of Yungay, the town at the base of Mount Huascarán, told Peck that the mountain could not be climbed. Peck hoped to prove them wrong. In 1904 she started up the mountain twice, only to be forced to turn back. The first time, her porter refused to work. The second time, a fierce blizzard caused her to return to Yungay.

Mountain climbers in the early 1900s

Mount Huascarán is a beautiful mountain in Peru.

Peck returned to Peru twice in 1906 to try again. Both climbs ended in failure because Peck had trouble with the people she had hired.

By 1908 Annie Peck had the money to try again. She hired two Swiss guides, Rudolf and Gabriel, and two porters. Halfway up the mountain, she discovered she had brought the wrong film. Without pictures, she couldn't prove that she had reached the peak. So, she sent one of the porters back to get the right film.

Next, Rudolf became ill and had to turn back. Gabriel did his best to cut steps in the ice wall alone. But the effort wore him out. Just two hours from the top, he stopped. He couldn't move another inch. Peck knew she couldn't possibly go on without Gabriel. She had no choice but to give up for the fifth time.

A Final Try

After just one day's rest in Yungay, Peck was ready to try for the sixth time. This time she hired four porters to carry all the food and equipment. Gabriel and Rudolf felt better, so she asked them to go, too.

The climb went smoothly at first. Peck's group made good time. Then one of the porters slipped off an ice bridge and into a deep crevasse. Luckily, he was tied to

Annie Smith Peck truly earned her title "Queen of the Climbers."

the same rope as Peck and Rudolf. They rescued him, but he dropped his pack into the crevasse. Inside the pack was the stove they needed for cooking food. Without it, they would have to quit.

To Peck's relief, Gabriel had a plan. Tying himself to a rope, he disappeared into the icy crevasse. After several long, scary minutes, he appeared with the pack and the stove. The climb continued.

Soon the peak was within view. Peck and Gabriel made plans for the final climb. While they weren't looking, Rudolf slipped away. At about 3 P.M. on September 2, 1908, Peck and Gabriel were ready to climb to the peak. At last, Peck would conquer the mountain. Suddenly, Rudolf appeared and announced that he had just been to the peak.

Peck was furious! As the leader, it was her right to be the first one to the summit. Still, this was Annie Smith Peck's day of **triumph**. She finally stood on the summit of Mount Huascarán. At the age of 58, she truly had earned the title "Queen of the Climbers."

USE WHAT YOU KNOW

Read and Remember — Choose the Answer

Draw a circle around the correct answer.

1. Which is one mountain that Peck climbed?

   Mount Mexico   Yungay   Matterhorn

2. What did Peck need to get before she could go on a climbing trip?

   a title   money   college classes

3. Who climbed Mount Huascarán with Annie Smith Peck?

   her parents   guides and porters   no one

4. How many times did Peck try to climb Mount Huascarán?

   two   six   twelve

5. What did Peck want to bring to the top of Mount Huascarán?

   a camera and film   a rock from Yungay   three flags

6. Who snuck away and reached the summit of Mount Huascarán before Peck?

   Rudolph   Gabriel   Shasta

Think About It — Find the Main Ideas

Underline the two most important ideas from the story.

1. Peck wanted to climb a mountain that no one else had ever climbed.

2. The people of Yungay were interested in what Peck was doing.

3. Peck never made it to the top of Mount Sorata.

4. One of Peck's porters dropped his pack into a crevasse.

5. Peck had problems with guides and porters during her climbs.

6. During a 1904 climb, a bad storm forced Peck to turn back.

Focus on Vocabulary — Crossword Puzzle

Use the clues to complete the puzzle. Choose from the words in dark print.

plunge	dismay	conquered	supported	equator
triumph	porters	altitude	failure	crevasses

Across

3. imaginary line around the middle of the world

5. fall suddenly

7. climbed to the top

9. height

10. people who carry supplies

Down

1. the act of not completing a goal or task

2. a great success

4. earned money to buy food and clothing

6. deep cracks in rock or ice

8. a feeling of fear

Hemispheres

Earth can be divided into **hemispheres**. The area north of the **equator** is the Northern Hemisphere. The area south of the equator is the Southern Hemisphere. Earth can also be divided into the Eastern Hemisphere and the Western Hemisphere. Annie Smith Peck climbed many mountains in different hemispheres. Study the map below. Write the answer to each question.

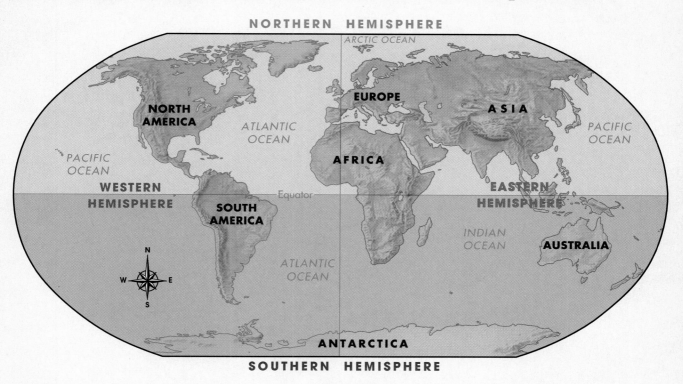

1. Is most of Asia in the Eastern or Western Hemisphere? _____

2. Is North America in the Eastern or Western Hemisphere? _____

3. The Matterhorn is in Europe. Is the Matterhorn in the Northern or Southern Hemisphere? _____

4. Mount Huascarán is in South America. Is Mount Huascarán in the Eastern or Western Hemisphere? _____

5. Name the two hemispheres that Australia is in. _____

_____

29

To Ski the Tallest Mountain

Yuichiro Miura loved to ski very fast. He said, "… to be the fastest skier in the world, I would trade my life."

Many people had thought that was just what Miura was doing when he put on his skis on May 7, 1970. They didn't think he would end the day alive. That was because Miura was not going to ski down an ordinary **slope**. He was going to ski down Mount Everest, the tallest mountain in the world.

A Crazy Plan

It was in the late 1960s that Miura first had the idea of skiing down Mount Everest. Although the plan sounded crazy, Miura was completely serious. He loved the thrill of racing down a mountain. To get the **ultimate** thrill, he decided to go to the tallest mountain. That meant traveling to Asia's Himalayan Mountains. Mount Everest is a part of the Himalayas. It is in the country of Nepal.

The peak of Mount Everest is 29,028 feet above **sea level**. Miura found a good slope that began at more than 26,000 feet. He planned to ski there.

Skiing fast would not be a problem on Mount Everest. The trail Miura picked was very steep. It had a length of about 6,000 feet. By the end of the trail, Miura would have dropped 3,000 feet in altitude. It would take him just six seconds to reach his top speed of almost 125 miles per hour. His problem would be slowing down.

At the bottom of the trail was a cliff that dropped straight down. Miura had to stop before reaching that.

He planned to stop by using a special brake system. He would wear a **parachute** on his back, opening it when he reached his top speed. The parachute would fill with air and slow him down. He had tried the parachute on a smaller mountain, Mount Fuji in Japan. The parachute had worked. With luck, it would work on Mount Everest, too.

Miura had to plan for other problems, as well. For instance, he had to climb up the mountain before he could ski down it. The climb itself would take weeks. There were many dangers. He might fall into a crevasse. He might slip on the ice or be killed by a rock **slide**.

Miura also had to think about the weather. Even on a good day, the temperature on Mount Everest is freezing. Fierce blizzards can begin at any moment.

None of these problems bothered Miura. He was determined to ski Mount Everest. He wanted the world to know what he was doing, so he planned to have people film the event. So the movie people had to climb the mountain, too. About 800 porters were needed to carry all the equipment up the mountain. Miura also needed guides, so he hired many Sherpas, people from an area of Nepal and of nearby China. Everyone needed food, clothing, and bedding. The cost of Miura's project would be about $3 million.

There was another cost to the project, one that went beyond dollars and cents. Six Sherpas died on the way up. They were killed when a wall of snow came crashing down on them. It was a loss that no one could have expected.

Movie people filming Miura

The Moment Arrives

Miura decided to continue the project. By May 7, he had reached his starting point. The cameras were in position. The temperature was ten **degrees** below zero. The wind was so strong that Miura had trouble

Miura loved to ski fast.

walking. However, it was not snowing, and the sky was clear. The time had come for him to ski.

Miura stood at the top of the steep, icy slope. He made sure his parachute was buckled on properly. He put on his helmet. He was well aware of the **risk** he was taking. In a few moments, he might be dead. He said, "If the parachute does not open within seven seconds, I will break the world speed-skiing record — and all my bones." Still, Miura gave a push and headed down the slope.

Facing Death

As Miura had hoped, he went faster than anyone had ever gone on skis. Six seconds into the run, he opened his parachute. But Miura didn't slow down. With a flash of **panic**, he realized the parachute wasn't working. He had forgotten just how thin the air was at this altitude. In such thin air, the parachute couldn't fill up properly. It just trailed along behind him, dragging uselessly on the ground.

"I am **utterly** out of control," Miura thought to himself. "I am saying good-by to my life."

At that point, Miura fell. His skis were ripped from his feet. His back and head banged on the ice. Farther and farther down the mountain he tumbled, still moving at a frightening speed. He was headed straight for the cliff at the bottom of the slope.

Suddenly, Miura crashed into one of the large rocks on the trail. That rock saved his life. Yuichiro Miura came to a stop just yards from the cliff at the bottom of the slope. He lay there, alive.

It took Miura a few seconds to realize that he had done it. He had skied down Mount Everest. Later, Miura said he thought the experience had changed him. It ended his desire to take great risks. As he put it, "Perhaps, having met the world of death, I have learned to **respect** it.

Miura said that skiing down Mount Everest changed him.

USE WHAT YOU KNOW

Read and Remember — Finish the Sentence

▲ **Circle the best ending for each sentence.**

1. Yuichiro Miura loved to ski _____.
fast   in the rain   through forests

2. To ski Mount Everest, Miura had to go to _____.
Japan   Europe   the Himalayas

3. Miura created a new way for skiers to _____.
climb   slow down   breathe

4. While skiing down Mount Everest, Miura _____.
became sick   fell   got lost

5. As he skied down the mountain, Miura thought about _____.
his children   making a movie   death

6. Miura came to a stop when he _____.
hit a rock   lost a ski   made a sharp turn

Write About It

▲ **Imagine you were one of the people filming Miura as he skied down Mount Everest. Write a short paragraph describing how you felt as you watched him ski.**

Focus on Vocabulary — Finish Up

Choose the correct word in dark print to complete each sentence.

ultimate	**sea level**	**utterly**	**panic**
parachute	**degrees**	**slide**	**respect**
risk	**slope**		

1. Ground that slants is a _____.

2. Temperature is measured in units called _____.

3. A sudden feeling of fear is _____.

4. _____ means greatest or last.

5. A rock _____ is a group of rocks and dirt tumbling down a mountain or hill.

6. A large piece of cloth that opens to catch wind and slow you down is a _____.

7. The average height of ocean water is _____.

8. To _____ is to think well of or have regard for.

9. To take a chance of getting hurt is to take a _____.

10. _____ means completely.

USE A MAP

Latitude and Longitude

You can find places on globes and maps by using lines. Lines that run east to west are called lines of **latitude**. Lines that run north to south are called lines of **longitude**. All the lines are marked using **degrees**, or °. Yuichiro Miura skied down Mount Everest. The mountain is at the 27°N latitude and the 87°N longitude. Study the map. Circle the answer that best completes each sentence below.

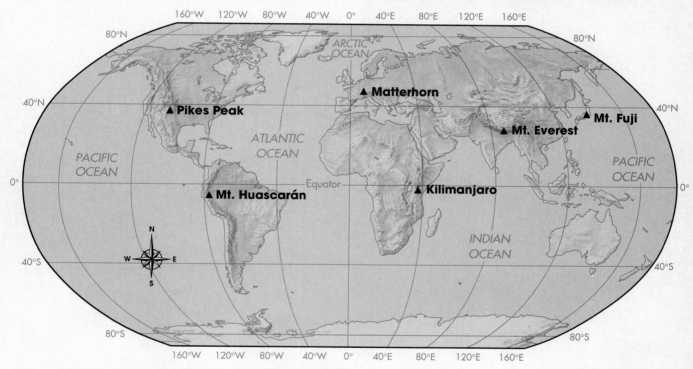

1. What is the latitude of Mount Fuji?

139°W   35°N   35°S

2. What is the longitude of Pikes Peak?

105°W   40°S   120°W

3. Which peak has a latitude of 3°S?

Pikes Peak   Matterhorn   Kilimanjaro

4. Which peak has a longitude of 77°W?

Matterhorn   Mount Fuji   Mount Huascarán

Nightmare
in the Sierras

Lauren Elder put on a wool skirt and high-heeled boots. She was going on a picnic. She and two friends planned to leave from Oakland, California. They were going to fly a small plane over the Sierra Nevada Mountains and into Death Valley. There, they would take pictures of **desert** flowers. Then they would have a picnic and fly home that same day. However, this trip turned out to be no picnic.

The Crash

It was April 26, 1976. Jay Fuller was the pilot. His girlfriend, Jean Noller, sat next to him. Lauren Elder happily climbed into the backseat of the small plane. She could see out of both windows. Once in the air, she began taking pictures of the wilderness below.

Soon, the plane was high in the Sierra Nevada Mountains. To clear the mountains, Fuller had to fly through a low point between two peaks. The low point he chose was near the top of 12,360-foot Mount Bradley. "Get ready for a fantastic view when we clear the **crest**," he called out to Elder. "There's going to be a desert valley on the other side."

They never made it through that low point. A sudden **air current** hit the plane. The blast of air knocked the plane down. When Elder looked ahead, all she saw was rock. A second later, the plane crashed into the mountain. Jay Fuller had missed the crest by just 15 feet. The broken plane stayed on a **ledge** on the mountain.

The crash broke Elder's left arm and put a deep cut in her right knee. It also knocked out several of her teeth. Jay Fuller had a deep cut in his head. His face was covered with blood. Jean Noller was even more seriously hurt. Her face was badly cut, and she was **unconscious**.

Elder and Fuller pulled Jean Noller out of the plane. They put a jacket on her to keep her warm. Suddenly, Noller's body began to jerk wildly. When Elder tried to hold her still, both women went sliding down the side of the mountain. Fuller rushed down and grabbed them. Together, he and Elder held onto Noller.

A Long, Deadly Night

After two hours, Fuller became too weak from his **injuries** to hold Noller any longer. Elder, with her broken arm, couldn't hold Noller by herself. When they let go, Noller's body slid another 120 feet down the slope. Elder knew that Jean Noller was dead.

Then Fuller told Elder that his stomach hurt. He seemed confused. Elder knew that if they were going to make it, she would have to take control.

With night coming, Elder and Fuller made a shelter in the tail section of the plane. Elder knew they had to build a fire nearby or risk freezing to death. She gathered loose paper. Then she lit the pile with gas from the plane. But in the thin air, the fire burned poorly.

Elder and Fuller couldn't keep the fire going. The rocks that had been under the fire were still warm, however. Elder thought that these rocks would keep their heat longer in the plane. So she carried them into the tail section. Fuller was too sick to help her. The hot rocks burned Elder's hands. She told herself that this was what she had to do to stay alive. The rocks helped keep them warm.

Lauren Elder

Lauren Elder stands in front of the Sierra Nevada Mountains.

Saving Her Own Life

Sometime during that night, Jay Fuller died. Elder's only hope was to climb down the mountain while she still had the strength to move. She would have to do it with a broken arm and in high-heeled boots.

First, Elder climbed the 15 feet to the summit. On the other side of the mountain was Owens Valley. There were small towns in the valley where people could help her. If Elder could get down there, she would be safe. But there was a problem. To get there, she would have to **descend** a long wall of ice and snow. The valley was a mile and a half below.

Elder's arm and mouth hurt, and she was hungry. She hadn't slept in 36 hours. Somehow, though, she managed to dig holes in the wall of ice and snow. Slowly, she crawled down, keeping her eyes on the wall. She feared that if she looked away, she would lose hope and give up.

At last, the wall grew less steep. It became possible to turn around, sit down, and slide from one rock to the next. Finally, Elder was at the bottom. She began to walk across the valley. Her boots filled with snow as she went. Still, she kept going.

Elder was very weak, cold, and tired. She was so **exhausted** that she even began to see things as she walked. She saw a row of houses. She saw a man in a white robe and a woman painting. She heard children laughing. None of these things were real. Sensing this, Elder made herself keep walking.

In time, the **landscape** turned from snow to stony fields. Elder came across a dry **riverbed**. She followed its course. Her hopes sank when it ended at a cliff. She was so tired. How was she ever going to climb down the 100-foot wall of rock?

Elder had come too far to turn around. So with her stomach flat against the rocks, Elder began to crawl down the cliff. She found tiny ledges for her feet. Slowly, she made it to the bottom.

It was dark when Elder finally stumbled into the tiny town of Independence, California. The sheriff rushed her to the hospital. Elder was tired, confused, and in pain, but she had made it. Against all odds, Lauren Elder was going to live.

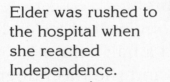

Elder was rushed to the hospital when she reached Independence.

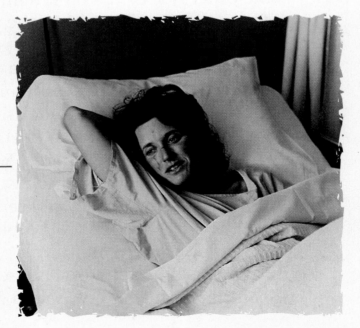

Read and Remember — Check the Events

🔺 **Place a check in front of the three sentences that tell what happened in the story.**

_____ **1.** The plane carrying Lauren Elder crashed into the side of a mountain.

_____ **2.** Jay Fuller and Jean Noller came to rescue Elder.

_____ **3.** Elder stayed warm by wrapping up in her sleeping bag.

_____ **4.** Elder climbed down a long wall of ice and snow.

_____ **5.** A blizzard trapped Elder on the mountain for three days.

_____ **6.** Elder saved herself by walking to a small town.

Think About It — Cause and Effect

🔺 **A cause is something that makes something else happen. What happens is called the effect. Match each cause with an effect. Write the letter on the correct blank. The first one is done for you.**

Cause	Effect
1. Elder and Fuller needed to stay warm, so ___c___	**a.** he couldn't help Elder carry the hot rocks.
2. Jay Fuller was badly injured, so _____	**b.** she was very tired.
3. Elder wanted to get to Owens Valley, so _____	**c.** Elder built a fire.
4. Elder had not slept in 36 hours, so _____	**d.** the sheriff rushed her to a hospital.
5. Elder reached Independence, so _____	**e.** she had to climb down the mountain.

USE WHAT YOU KNOW

Focus on Vocabulary — Finish the Paragraphs

Use the words in dark print to complete the paragraphs. Reread the paragraphs to be sure they make sense.

crest	**air current**	**unconscious**	**landscape**
desert	**descend**	**riverbed**	**injuries**
exhausted	**ledge**		

Lauren Elder planned to have a picnic in the (1)_____ of Death Valley. She was flying there with friends when a sudden (2)_____ made the plane drop. The plane could not clear the (3)_____ of the mountain in front of it. The plane crashed, falling onto a (4)_____ that was sticking out not far from the top of the mountain.

All three people in the plane had serious (5)_____. One woman was (6)_____ and did not know what was going on around her. After a night on the mountain, only Elder was still alive. To reach safety, she had to (7)_____ the icy mountain to the valley below.

As she walked across the valley, Elder saw the (8)_____ around her change. She began to walk along a dry (9)_____. By this time, she was very weak and (10)_____. But she kept going, until finally she reached the town of Independence, California.

Map Keys

Maps use different symbols or colors. A **map key** tells what the symbols or colors mean. This map shows the area where Lauren Elder's plane crashed. Study the map and map key. Write the answer to each question below.

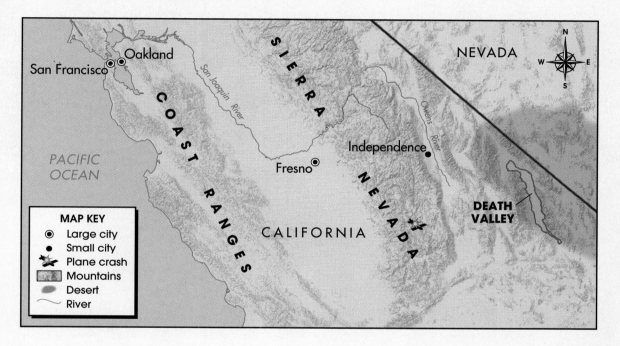

1. Draw the symbol for river. _____

2. Is the symbol for capital city shown on the map key? _____

3. Is Independence a small city or a large city? _____

4. What two mountain ranges are shown on the map? _____

_____

5. Did the plane crash occur in the desert? _____

6. Which river flows just east of Independence? _____

A Climb to Remember

Arlene Blum said, "We knew there was danger on Annapurna.... We just didn't know how much danger."

Blum was the leader of an all-woman team that in 1978 set out to climb Annapurna. This 26,504-foot mountain is part of the Himalayas in Nepal. By 1978, 13 teams had tried to climb the dangerous mountain. Only four teams had made it to the top. Nine people had died trying.

A Dangerous Mountain

One reason Annapurna is so hard to climb is that the snow on it is very **unstable**. The snow moves, settles, and then moves again. This often leads to an **avalanche**, a huge wave of snow tumbling down the mountain.

Another problem is the icy side of the mountain. Climbers face huge walls of ice that are at different **angles**. Also, climbers often have to cross narrow **ridges**. Some ridges are only a foot wide, with huge drops on both sides.

Still, Blum and nine other women felt ready for the challenge. They wanted to be the first Americans to reach the summit of Annapurna.

The group hired Sherpas to guide them up and down the mountain. These people lived in the **region** and were used to climbing in the Himalayas. The women also hired many porters.

On August 28, 1978, the women reached their base camp at 14,200 feet on Annapurna. The sky was clear.

They could see the icy peak nearly two-and-a-half miles straight up. They knew that the climb was not going to be easy. In fact, there was a sad **reminder** nearby. It was a stone with the names of seven of the nine climbers who had died on Annapurna.

Climbing a very tall mountain such as Annapurna takes a long time. So camps have to be set up along the way. Food and supplies are brought up from a lower camp to a higher one. Some members of the group stay back at each camp to cook, fix equipment, and run the radio. They use the radio to talk with the climbers.

By September 15, the women had set up the first two camps, Camps 1 and 2. They made plans to set up Camp 3. It would be at 21,000 feet. To get there, they would have to cross Dutch Rib, a very narrow ridge. The ridge drops off on both sides. Also, the area is hit often by avalanches. As Blum crossed the ridge, she mumbled to herself, "If I die, I die."

Close Calls

On September 26, Blum wrote in her journal, "It's really getting scary." That day an avalanche rushed

Arlene Blum poses with her team.

An avalanche rushed by one of the camps.

toward the women. They had to run to get out of the way. Luckily, wrote Blum, "the moving snow stopped just above us." Then they heard the roar of another avalanche. Again, it stopped before it reached them.

The Sherpas were spooked by the avalanches. They said it wasn't worth the risk. The Sherpas decided to quit. They agreed to come back only after Blum promised them more money.

The avalanches shook Blum's **confidence**. She began to have doubts about continuing. Still, none of the women gave up. On October 8, they set up Camp 4 at 23,200 feet. Even with the dangers, they were slowly making their way to the top.

Triumph and Loss

On October 14, three women and three Sherpas set up Camp 5. It was just 2,300 feet below the summit. The next day they would go to the top. Irene Miller, Vera Komarkova, Piro Kramar, and the Sherpas got up very early. Then Kramar saw that the tip of one finger was frozen. She ran back into her tent to warm it up. At last, she decided not to go. "I'd rather lose the summit than my finger," she said.

Miller, Komarkova, and two of the Sherpas started climbing at 7 A.M. At this altitude the air is very thin.

Arlene Blum carved the names of Chadwick and Watson on the stone.

Every step was **agony**. Each person had to take six breaths after each step. The snow was almost to their waists. Finally, at 3:30 P.M. they reached the summit. They placed the flags of the United States and Nepal in the snow and hugged each other.

On October 17, a second group headed for the top. They were Alison Chadwick, Vera Watson, and a Sherpa. But the Sherpa became ill, so the two women decided to risk going alone. Back at Camp 2, Blum waited all day for them to report their **progress** by radio. Evening came, but there was still no word.

The next morning Blum and the rest of the team looked out across the mountain. There was no sign of the two women. Blum sent two Sherpas to look for them. The Sherpas found their bodies still roped together at the bottom of a cliff. It seemed that one of the women had slipped, dragging the other woman 1,500 feet down an icy slope. What had been a great triumph now turned to sadness.

Later, the team carved the names of Chadwick and Watson below the other seven names on the stone at the base camp. Alison Chadwick and Vera Watson, whose bodies could not be **recovered**, would always remain with Annapurna.

USE WHAT YOU KNOW

Read and Remember — Choose the Answer

▲ **Draw a circle around the correct answer.**

1. Before Blum's group, how many Americans had reached the top of Annapurna?

   ten   two   none

2. What danger did Blum's team face?

   avalanches   floods   bears

3. What did Blum have to give the Sherpa guides to keep them from quitting?

   more food   more money   more ropes

4. What did two of the climbers place at the top of Annapurna?

   tents   flags   radios

5. How did Blum try to contact the missing climbers?

   by telephone   by radio   with hand signals

Write About It

▲ **Imagine you were a member of Blum's team. Write a letter to a friend, describing how you felt as you left Annapurna.**

Dear _____,

_____

_____

_____

_____

_____

_____

Focus on Vocabulary — Match Up

Match each word with its meaning. Write the correct letter on the blank.

_____ **1.** unstable

_____ **2.** avalanche

_____ **3.** angles

_____ **4.** ridges

_____ **5.** region

_____ **6.** reminder

_____ **7.** confidence

_____ **8.** agony

_____ **9.** progress

_____ **10.** recovered

a. different positions

b. a way to remember something

c. not firm

d. long, narrow parts of mountains

e. brought back

f. a wall of snow sliding out of control

g. trust in one's abilities

h. movement toward a goal

i. an area of land

j. great pain

Countries

Some maps give information about countries. Thin lines are used to show the **borders** between countries. The map key explains what symbols are used on the map. Arlene Blum and her team climbed Annapurna in Nepal, Asia. This map shows Nepal and the countries near it. Study the map and the map key. Write the answer to each question.

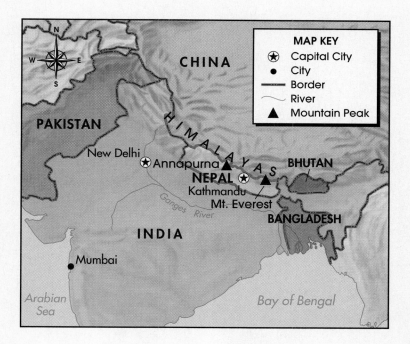

1. What is the capital city of Nepal? _____

2. Which two countries share a border with Nepal? _____

_____

3. Which country is just west of Bangladesh? _____

4. In which country is the city of Mumbai? _____

5. Which two peaks of the Himalayas are shown on the map? _____

_____

6. Does the Ganges River flow through Nepal? _____

A Killer Storm

It sounded like an exciting trip to the students from Oregon Episcopal School. They would reach Oregon's beautiful Mount Hood by 2 A.M. They would hike to the top, turn around, and be back before dark that day. The trip would let them use some of the climbing skills that they had been learning. Besides, for the past 35 years, students at the school had been making this climb. What could possibly go wrong?

A Storm Moves In

Mount Hood is climbed by thousands of people each year. But it can be a very unfriendly place. It has an **elevation** of 11,235 feet. That is high enough for bad weather to blow in without warning.

Although clouds covered Mount Hood on May 12, 1986, the trip continued as planned. The 15 teenagers were excited as they headed on a bus to Mount Hood. One parent, two teachers, and two expert climbers went with them. The group drove to Timberline Lodge, which was about 6,000 feet up the mountain. There, they prepared for their climb to the summit.

The group set out at 2 A.M. Within an hour they were climbing in strong winds and blowing snow. After ascending just 500 feet, 15-year-old Hilary Spray and her mother Sharon turned back. They were worried about the weather. "This climb is not worth your life," Sharon told her daughter.

Soon after that, 15-year-old Courtney Boatsman got a creepy feeling. She later said it was "like a voice saying, 'Go down.'" Boatsman turned back, and so did three other teenagers. One of the expert climbers got sick and also returned to the lodge.

So three adults and ten students slowly worked their way up the south **face** of the mountain. As they climbed, the wind grew stronger. By afternoon, it was blowing at 60 miles an hour. The **wind-chill factor** was 50 degrees below zero. When snow started to fall, the climbers could barely see one another. They were in the middle of a blizzard.

The climbers could not tell how close they were to the summit. Ralph Summers, the expert climber, thought that they were within 500 feet. But it didn't matter. The storm was getting worse. Summers knew that they had to get down off the mountain, fast.

Digging In

By the time the group got down to 8,300 feet, one boy was showing signs of **hypothermia**. His body

Mount Hood is beautiful and dangerous.

temperature was dropping very low. Others were suffering from the cold, too. "People were shaking and shivering," remembered 17-year-old Molly Schula. Yet everyone tried to stay calm. They had all been trained for such **emergencies**. Schula said, "we decided to dig in."

With Ralph Summers directing them, the students and teachers dug a snow cave. It took them about two hours. Then they climbed in, hoping to stay warm.

Although the cave got the group out of the wind, it was far too small for 13 people. Then, the heat from their bodies began to melt the cave floor. The climbers were soon sitting in ice-cold water.

All night the group huddled there. By morning, the storm was as fierce as ever. Ralph Summers feared that they all would die before the weather cleared. So he decided to go for help. Molly Schula **volunteered** to go with him.

Summers and Schula said goodbye to the others. "I told them we would keep walking until we found help or died," remembered Summers. Then, with Summers' **compass** to guide them, he and Schula began to head slowly down the mountain. The wind was whipping snow in all directions. Schula later said, "I kept thinking I would never get home and see my mother again."

Molly Schula

Rescue Efforts

After three-and-a-half hours, Summers and Schula made it to safety. By then, **rescuers** were already out searching the mountain. All day the blizzard continued. Though the rescuers tried hard, they did not find the snow cave.

The next day, the weather improved. That morning searchers found three of the students halfway down the mountain. Like Summers and Schula, they had left the cave to seek help. Sadly, they did not survive. Their still bodies were found covered with ice.

Rescuers rushed Thompson in a helicopter to a nearby hospital.

The rescuers continued. By evening, the last six students and two teachers were still missing. The next day, the rescuers tried again. This time they used 12-foot poles to poke around in the snow. At last, late in the day, one pole hit a backpack. They began to dig.

As the rescuers dug down, they heard soft moans. Quickly, they shoveled down to the cave. There, under more than four feet of snow, lay the eight climbers. Sixteen-year-old Giles Thompson and 15-year-old Brinton Clark had their eyes open and were still breathing. Their hearts were barely beating. Their body temperatures were **dangerously** low. The other six people appeared to be frozen to death.

The eight climbers were rushed to nearby hospitals in helicopters. Doctors began to warm their bodies slowly to a normal temperature. But only Brinton Clark and Giles Thompson lived. Thompson's legs were so badly frozen that doctors had to cut them off below the knees.

The world was shocked and sad about what had happened to the group. The death of the nine climbers was the worst **tragedy** in Mount Hood's history. It was a chilling reminder of the power of nature.

USE WHAT YOU KNOW

Read and Remember — Finish the Sentence

▲ **Circle the best ending for each sentence.**

1. The students were near Mount Hood's summit when a _____.
   tree fell   blizzard moved in   plane crashed

2. Thirteen people spent the night in a cold and wet _____.
   tent   snow cave   school bus

3. Ralph Summers and Molly Schula went to get _____.
   help   some rope   more food

4. The rescuers did not find any of the climbers until _____.
   night   the weather improved   a helicopter came

5. Rescuers poked around in the snow with _____.
   long poles   tree branches   bright lights

6. Giles Thompson and Brinton Clark both _____.
   stayed home   walked to safety   survived

Think About It — Fact or Opinion

▲ A **fact** is a true statement. An **opinion** is a statement that tells what a person thinks. Write **F** beside each statement that is a fact. Write **O** beside each statement that is an opinion.

_____ 1. People should not be allowed to climb Mount Hood.

_____ 2. Hilary Spray and her mother turned back early.

_____ 3. The blizzard made it hard to see one another.

_____ 4. Ralph Summers feared that they would all die.

_____ 5. Rescuers should have used whistles to find the climbers.

_____ 6. It was foolish to climb Mount Hood in bad weather.

USE WHAT YOU KNOW

Focus on Vocabulary — Make a Word

▲ Choose a word in dark print to complete each sentence. Write the letters of the word on the blanks. When you are finished, the letters in the circles will tell what was used to help rescue the Mount Hood climbers.

elevation   **compass**   **volunteered**   **face**
dangerously   **hypothermia**   **tragedy**   **rescuers**
emergencies   **wind-chill**

1. One boy's low body temperature meant he was in danger of _____.

   ⃝ _ _ _ _ _ _ _ _ _ _

2. Many _____ looked for the missing climbers.

   ⃝ _ _ _ _ _ _ _ _

3. Schula _____ to go with Summers to get help.

   ⃝ _ _ _ _ _ _ _ _ _ _

4. The _____ factor made the temperature 50 degrees below zero.

   ⃝ _ _ _ _ - _ _ _ _ _

5. The group climbed the mountain's south _____.

   ⃝ _ _ _ _

6. Clark's body temperature was falling _____ low.

   ⃝ _ _ _ _ _ _ _ _ _ _ _

7. Summers had brought an instrument called a _____.

   ⃝ _ _ _ _ _ _ _

8. Mount Hood's _____ is 11,235 feet.

   ⃝ _ _ _ _ _ _ _ _ _

9. It was a terrible _____ that the students died.

   ⃝ _ _ _ _ _ _ _

10. The students thought that they could handle _____.

   ⃝ _ _ _ _ _ _ _ _ _ _ _

Distance Scale

Mount Hood is about fifty miles from Portland, Oregon. On a map, use a **distance scale** to find the distance between two places. This map's distance scale shows that 1 inch of the map stands for 100 miles of land. Use a ruler to measure the distances on the map. Circle the correct answer to each question.

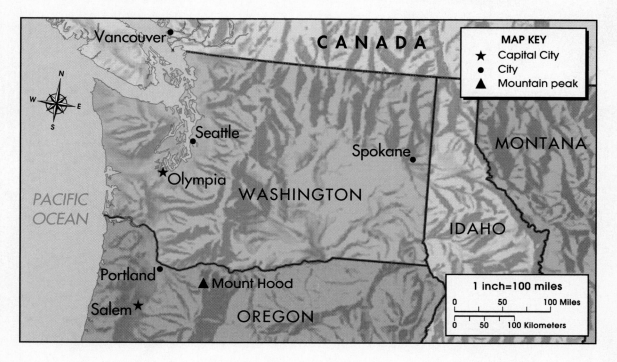

1. How many inches are between Portland and Spokane on the map?

   $1\frac{1}{2}$ inches   2 inches   3 inches

2. What is the actual distance between Portland and Spokane?

   150 miles   300 miles   350 miles

3. What is the actual distance between Olympia and Salem?

   75 miles   150 miles   200 miles

4. Which place is about 225 miles from Seattle?

   Vancouver   Mount Hood   Spokane

Volcano!

It was a quiet day in the country of Colombia in South America. As the sun came up on January 14, 1993, the Galeras **volcano** looked very peaceful. But at 1:43 P.M., the volcano gave a sudden roar. A huge stream of gas, rocks, and ash came flying out of its center. People on the volcano had little time to act. For nine of them, the sudden **eruption** meant death.

No Warning

The eruption was not the first time in recent years that the volcano had blown up. There had been a small eruption just six months earlier. In fact, Galeras was the most active volcano in Colombia.

Galeras lies in the southwest corner of Colombia. Thirteen miles from Galeras is Pasto, a city of 300,000 people. At an elevation of 13,680 feet, Galeras towers over the city of Pasto. But until 1993, people in Pasto were not worried about the volcano. No one in the town had been killed by an eruption in 500 years. People in Pasto knew that Galeras exploded from time to time, but that didn't bother them. In fact, the volcano seemed to be good for business. **Tourists** came from all over the country to visit it.

Scientists came, too. In fact, 75 scientists from around the world gathered at Galeras in January 1993. They came to study the volcano and to get samples of gases from inside it. By doing this, they hoped to **predict** when the next eruption might be.

Scientists often study Galeras to learn more about volcanoes.

On January 14, some of these scientists climbed to the top of the volcano. Two scientists then used ropes to lower themselves down into the **crater** of the volcano. There, they began their work. Other scientists stayed up on the **rim**. Among them were Florida professor Andrew McFarlane and Arizona professor Stanley Williams.

Suddenly, as McFarlane later said, "there was a loud boom." He looked up. A dark cloud came shooting up over the top of the crater. "For just a second, it was hard to tell how serious it was," he said. "But we knew it wasn't good, and we started running."

A stream of deadly gas was shooting out of the volcano. The temperature of the gas was more than 1,100 degrees. Rocks and ash flew one-and-a-half miles into the air. A Colombian tourist who saw the eruption said, "The volcano seemed to take a big breath, first sucking in air, then exploding."

Trying to Get Away

The eruption caught everyone by surprise. The two scientists inside the crater were killed right away by the hot gas. Three scientists up on the rim also were burned to death. Three Colombian tourists on another part of the volcano died in the eruption, too.

McFarlane and Williams tried to get to a safe spot. So did some Colombians who were near them. McFarlane said, "Within seconds, these blocks of hot rock were falling all around us." One rock hit him. Then McFarlane saw a Colombian scientist get crushed by another of these flying rocks. The **death toll** was nine people. McFarlane said, "At that point, it seemed very unlikely that any of us were going to get out alive."

The rock that had hit McFarlane had struck his head. Blood poured down his face. Beside him, Williams was hit, too. Williams fell to the ground with a broken jaw and two broken ankles. McFarlane tried to pick him up and carry him. He couldn't do it. He later said, "I was dazed… and I was too weak to carry him, so I just kept running."

Again and again, McFarlane slipped on the ground, which was now covered with hot ashes. He had burns on his hands. He found himself gasping for breath in the thin air. At last, he just couldn't go any farther. He fell to the ground, exhausted.

Stanley Williams survived the Galeras eruption, but he had broken bones.

To the Rescue

Members of the Red Cross, an **organization** that helps people in emergencies, rushed to Galeras. They ran to help the eruption's many **victims**, including McFarlane and Williams. The heat from the eruption had melted the backpack Williams was wearing. His sunglasses also had melted. Papers he had been carrying in his pocket had burned up. Yet somehow Williams, like McFarlane, had survived.

Later, scientists said no one could have known about the Galeras eruption before it happened. Experts also pointed out that the eruption really was quite small. A bigger one would have put the whole town of Pasto in danger. But any eruption is serious when people are hurt or killed. Today, tourists are no longer allowed to visit the volcano.

The people of Pasto know that someday their town might be in great danger from Galeras. Yet few move away. But those people who survived the eruption that day in 1993 will never forget the power of the volcano or the fear they felt. Said McFarlane, "Nature doesn't care. There was no **mercy** out there."

Someday, the city of Pasto might be in danger from a Galeras eruption.

Read and Remember — Check the Events

🔺 **Place a check in front of the three sentences that tell what happened in the story.**

_____ **1.** Scientists caused the volcano to blow up.

_____ **2.** Galeras erupted without warning.

_____ **3.** The city of Pasto was destroyed when the volcano exploded.

_____ **4.** Andrew McFarlane escaped the eruption without getting hurt.

_____ **5.** Some people were killed in the eruption.

_____ **6.** A huge stream of gas flew out of Galeras.

Write About It

🔺 **Do you think tourists should still be allowed on Galeras? Write a short paragraph telling why or why not.**

USE WHAT YOU KNOW

Focus on Vocabulary — Crossword Puzzle

Use the clues to complete the puzzle. Choose from the words in dark print.

volcano   **crater**   **rim**   **predict**

death toll   **victims**   **mercy**   **eruption**

tourists   **organization**

Across

1. number of people who died

4. a mountain that can explode with hot gases or rocks

7. people who have been hurt or killed

8. outer edge

10. when something explodes

Down

2. group of people who meet for a purpose

3. people who visit a place for fun

5. a hollow area

6. to guess what is going to happen

9. kindness

Latitude and Longitude

Lines that run east to west around Earth are called lines of **latitude**. Lines that run north to south are called lines of **longitude**. All the lines are measured in **degrees**, or °. Latitude and longitude can be used together to show a place's location. For example, the Galeras volcano is at 1°N, 77°W. The latitude is written first, then the longitude. Study the map of volcanoes. Circle the answer that best completes each sentence.

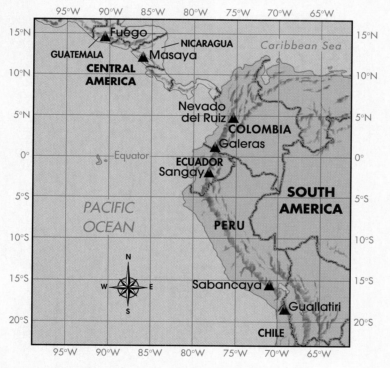

1. The volcano that has a latitude of 18°S is _____.

Sangay   Masaya   Guallatiri

2. The volcano that has a longitude of 78°W is _____.

Sabancaya   Sangay   Nevado del Ruiz

3. The latitude of Fuego is _____.

91°N   14°N   14°S

4. The volcano at 5°N, 76°W is _____.

Masaya   Guallatiri   Nevado del Ruiz

Breaking the Record

limber Mike Vining said, Todd Huston "had no… **mountaineering** experience. He had no winter camping experience. He had no idea what he was doing." Yet on May 20, 1994, Todd Huston set out to climb Alaska's Denali Mountain. Denali is the highest mountain in North America. It can be hard for the most experienced climbers. For Huston, it was even harder. That's because Todd Huston has only one leg.

Great Changes

When Huston was 14, he was in a bad boating accident. Doctors had to **amputate** his right leg below the knee. Before the accident, Huston had played sports. Afterwards, though, he gave them up. His **artificial** leg made it difficult to run or jump. It took a lot of work just to walk.

After college, Huston began a career helping other people with **physical disabilities**. Then in 1993, he learned about the 50 Peaks Project. Its leaders were forming a mountain-climbing team. Everyone on the team had a physical disability. The goal was to climb the highest point in every American state.

A man named Adrian Crane had already done that. However, Crane did not have a physical disability. Besides, it had taken him 101 days to do it. The team planned to beat that time. Huston eagerly joined.

Before Huston could climb anything, he had to get in shape. He did that by running. At first, he could barely run 20 feet. He worked his way up to 100 feet, then to a mile. It wasn't easy. Often, he fell. Sometimes his artificial leg, which was made of wood and plastic, broke. Still, Huston **persisted**. By the end of three months, he could run 12 miles.

Huston also worked to build climbing skills. He joined a gym with a climbing wall. He even got an artificial leg made just for climbing.

Summit America

The 50 Peaks Project later fell apart, but Huston kept going on his own. Huston thought that he could beat Crane's record. He called his new project Summit America.

Denali Mountain

In some states, reaching the highest point wouldn't be hard. In Florida, the highest point is only 345 feet above sea level. In Delaware, it is in the middle of a busy city road. Mississippi's highest point, Woodall, is called a mountain. But Woodall Mountain is only 806 feet high.

Still, Huston would face some big challenges to reach his goal. He would need to climb several mountains over 13,000 feet. Hardest of all would be Denali Mountain. Denali is also known as Mount McKinley. The mountain is 20,320 feet high. It is very cold near the top. In fact, Denali is one of the coldest mountains in the **Northern Hemisphere**.

Denali has many dangerous storms. Most people who try to climb it turn back before getting to the top. Some climbers don't make it off the mountain at all. Over the years, many people have lost their lives to Denali.

Huston talked over his plans with guide Whit Rambach, who would go with him. They decided to start with Denali. It was the climb that would take the most time. Also, if any mountain was going to **defeat** them, it was going to be Denali.

Reaching the Top

Huston and Rambach were ready to begin Summit America. They flew to Alaska. Climbers Adrian Crane, who had set the original record, and Mike Vining went with them. Once on Denali, they set up a base camp at 7,000 feet. Huston said, "From there, we began hiking up the mountain."

Often, they got terribly cold. "It was so cold, it actually snowed inside the tent," Huston remembered. His breath would rise to the top of the tent. Then it would turn to snow and fall back down on him. "We couldn't take our gloves off for more than 15 seconds or our hands would have frozen," Huston said.

The wind was also very strong. It usually blew around 40 miles an hour. During storms, it "got up to 70 miles an hour," said Huston. "All you could hear was the crush of snow and ice."

As Huston climbed up Denali, he met climbers coming down. Many of them had given up because of the stormy weather. Yet Huston kept going. But there were problems. It took more energy to climb with an artificial leg. Also, he had to go slower. The artificial leg rubbed against him, causing pain. "By the end of the day, he had extra pain that the rest of us didn't have to deal with," said Mike Vining.

Todd Huston said it was so cold that sometimes it snowed inside the tent.

At 16,000 feet, Huston and his climbing partners reached a 2,000-foot wall of ice. They climbed it using ropes and **ice axes**. On June 1, they made the final push to reach the summit.

By then, Huston was struggling. The high altitude meant that there wasn't much **oxygen** in the air. Huston had to rest between every step. "I just kept telling myself over and over: Three breaths, step, stop and rest." Again and again he fell down. His partners didn't say a word. They just waited quietly while he struggled to his feet.

"I have to admit, I thought about quitting more than once," Huston said. He didn't give up, though. At last, he stood on top of Denali. He had climbed the hardest mountain in the United States.

Todd Huston went on to reach all the other high points in the United States. He did it in just 67 days, beating Crane's record. But for Huston, climbing mountains was more than just an adventure. He said, "Through climbing, I am **representing** the struggle in all of us."

Huston climbed all of the highest points in the United States.

USE WHAT YOU KNOW

Read and Remember — Choose the Answer

Draw a circle around the correct answer.

1. What did Huston do before climbing any mountains?

   He got in shape.   He flew to each state.   He learned to ski.

2. What did Huston call his project?

   Summit America   Denali Climb   Highest Peaks

3. What was the first mountain that Huston climbed?

   Woodall Mountain   Mount Delaware   Denali

4. Whose record did Huston want to beat?

   Adrian Crane's   Mike Vining's   Whit Rambach's

5. What problem did Huston's group face?

   high winds   blinding sunlight   rain

6. What did Huston get for his climbing trips?

   a special artificial leg   a telephone   firewood

Think About It — Find The Main Ideas

Underline the two most important ideas from the story.

1. As a child, Todd Huston played sports.

2. Some states do not have tall mountains.

3. People with physical disabilities can climb mountains if they want to.

4. It snowed inside Huston's tent.

5. Denali is also called Mount McKinley.

6. Todd Huston worked hard to climb Denali.

Focus on Vocabulary — Finish the Paragraphs

Use the words in dark print to complete the paragraphs. Reread the paragraphs to be sure they make sense.

Northern Hemisphere	**oxygen**	**amputate**	**ice axes**
physical disabilities	**defeat**	**persisted**	**representing**
mountaineering	**artificial**		

As a boy, Todd Huston was in a bad boating accident. Doctors had to (1)_____ his leg from the knee down. He was fitted with an (2)_____ leg. Huston went on to help others who also had (3)_____. Then in 1993, he joined a mountain-climbing team. At that time, Huston knew little about the sport of (4)_____. But he was willing to learn.

The first mountain Huston tried to climb was Denali. It is one of the coldest mountains in the (5)_____. There is not much (6)_____ in the thin air near the peak.

Huston's group used sharp tools called (7)_____ to help them climb the walls of ice. At times, Huston was worried that the mountain might (8)_____ him. Still, he (9)_____, until at last he stood on the summit. Huston thought others could follow his example to face their own challenges. He said, "Through climbing, I am (10)_____ the struggle in all of us."

Distance Scale

On a map, use a **distance scale** to find the distance between two places. On this map of Alaska, the distance scale shows that 1 inch of the map stands for 300 miles of land. Use a ruler to measure the distances on the map. Circle the correct answer to each question.

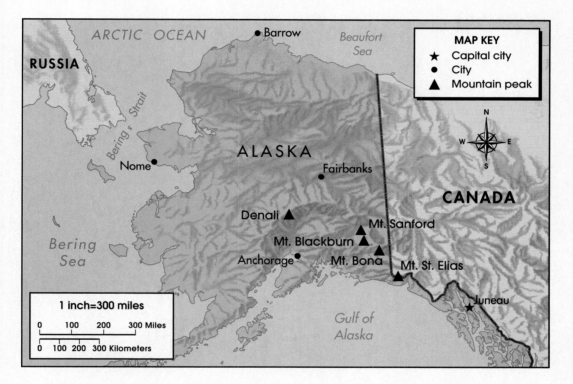

1. How many inches are between Juneau and Denali on the map?

   1 inch   2 inches   3 inches

2. What is the actual distance between Juneau and Denali?

   100 miles   300 miles   600 miles

3. What is the actual distance between Mount St. Elias and Anchorage?

   100 miles   150 miles   300 miles

4. Which city is about 525 miles from Fairbanks?

   Anchorage   Nome   Juneau

Against All Hope

Juan Reyes was looking forward to Christmas 1995. The whole family would be gathering in his **hometown** of Cali, Colombia. On December 20, Juan and others of his family went to the airport to get Juan's brother Mauricio. But the plane didn't arrive. Then the family heard that the plane had crashed into San Jose Mountain, forty miles from the airport. Juan said, "My whole world fell apart at that very moment."

Flying Too Low

Flight 965 seemed fine as it flew away from Miami, Florida, and entered the **Southern Hemisphere**. But something went wrong as it neared Cali, Colombia's second-largest **metropolitan** area. The airplane dropped to 9,000 feet. That was too low to clear the South American mountain range known as the Andes. In fact, the plane was headed right for 12,000-foot San Jose Mountain.

The pilots tried to bring the plane back up. But they couldn't do it. The plane crashed into the mountain. Most of the 164 passengers **aboard** were killed right away. Only four people survived. One of them was Mauricio Reyes, Juan's brother.

The crash knocked Mauricio out. When he woke up, it was dark and cold, and he was in agony. His back and face were broken in many places. His legs and chest hurt. He was covered with cuts. Next to him, a woman named Mercedes Ramirez also was hurt but alive. A little farther away lay Gonzalo Dussan and his six-year-old daughter Michelle. They were the only other **survivors**.

Mauricio hurt too much to move. He lay there, moaning softly. His only hope was that rescuers would find him before he died in this **remote** spot, far from a city.

Back at the airport, Juan was filled with **grief**. "I could not believe that my brother, the youngest child in our family, had died on his way home for Christmas," he said. Families of other victims were upset. "People were screaming, they were hugging, they were on their knees," said Juan. "It was terrible."

Then Juan saw rescue workers getting ready to go to San Jose Mountain. He asked to go with them. They agreed, and Juan prepared to go to the site.

The group rushed to the mountain. At 4 A.M., they began climbing up to where the plane had crashed. They had to cut their way through thick bushes. Soon, they were cold and thirsty. Juan didn't care. All his thoughts were on Mauricio. At one point, he turned to another rescuer. He said, "If you see a man who looks like me, it's my brother."

A plane similar to Flight 965

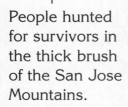

People hunted for survivors in the thick brush of the San Jose Mountains.

Rescuers carried one of the victims of the Flight 965 crash.

A Strange Feeling

For three hours the group climbed. They had no way of knowing if they were heading in the right direction. At last they met a man who lived nearby. He told them to keep going. He pointed higher up the mountain. "That's the way," he said.

One of the rescuers, John Fernando Bueno, didn't think so. He had a strange feeling that he should look somewhere else. Bueno took off by himself. He carried only a compass and a radio. The radio soon went dead. "No battery, no equipment, no nothing," he later said. "But I just moved on."

Bueno's **hunch** was right. By 9 A.M. he reached the far side of the mountain. He met soldiers who also were looking for the crash site. He moved past them onto a forested mountain ridge. There he came upon what was left of Flight 965.

It was a terrible sight. The plane had broken into hundreds of pieces. Clothing hung from the trees. Suitcases, toys, and books covered the ground. Bodies lay everywhere. As Bueno stared at the **wreckage**, he heard moans. That's when he knew a few people had survived the crash.

Bueno shouted out to the soldiers he had met. They came running. Quickly, they radioed for help.

Incredible Joy

When Juan Reyes and the other rescuers neared the crash site, Juan slowed down. He had no hope that his brother was still alive. Then someone came running up to him, screaming wildly.

"He was calling to me to come down," said Juan. The man yelled, "Sir, come quickly, come quickly. There is a man here who looks just like you."

"I ran as fast as I could," said Juan. "There, lying unconscious and bleeding, was my brother." Juan could barely believe it. "I can't describe the feeling," he later told people. He said that it was a "beautiful... miracle."

A rescue helicopter came. It could not land because of high winds. Instead, a basket for carrying people was sent down. One by one, the survivors were placed in it and pulled up into the helicopter. Then the helicopter took off for the hospital.

The families of the four survivors were thrilled to hear the news. Andres Reyes, a brother of Mauricio and Juan, said words that echoed the feelings of all his family. He said, "After all I've cried, what **incredible** joy."

This photo of Mauricio Reyes (right) and his brother Andres (left) was taken before the crash.

USE WHAT YOU KNOW

Read and Remember — Finish the Sentence

Circle the best ending for each sentence.

1. Flight 965 crashed into a mountain in the _____.
   Rockies   Andes   Alps

2. On the plane was Juan Reyes's _____.
   father   wife   brother

3. To get to the crash site, rescuers had to go through _____.
   deep water   thick bushes   city streets

4. John Fernando Bueno had a feeling he should _____.
   look somewhere else   turn off his radio   give up

5. When Mauricio Reyes was found, he was _____.
   walking   badly hurt   helping other victims

Write About It

Imagine you were a newspaper reporter. Write a short article about the crash of Flight 965. Tell who, what, when, where, and why in your article.

Focus on Vocabulary — Find the Meaning

Read each sentence. Circle the best meaning for the word or words in dark print.

1. The whole family would be gathering in Juan's **hometown**.

   place where someone grew up   large house   big city

2. The plane seemed fine as it entered the **Southern Hemisphere**.

   airport   lower half of the world   country of Columbia

3. Cali is Columbia's second-largest **metropolitan** area.

   city   hospital   place for playing music

4. Most of the 164 passengers **aboard** were killed right away.

   underneath   on the plane   waiting in line

5. There were only four **survivors**.

   people who stayed alive   families   helpers

6. Mauricio hoped rescuers would find him in this **remote** spot.

   dark   cold   far away

7. Juan Reyes was filled with **grief**.

   great sadness   excitement   hunger

8. John Fernando Bueno's **hunch** was right.

   book   friend   guess

9. As Bueno stared at the **wreckage**, he heard moans.

   broken pieces from a crash   group of trees   ground

10. Andres said, "After all I've cried, what **incredible** joy."

    little   amazing   late

Countries

Some maps give information about countries. Thin lines are used to show the **borders** between countries. The map key explains what symbols are used on the map. This map shows Colombia and other countries in the northern part of South America. Study the map and the map key. Write the answer to each question.

1. What is the capital city of Bolivia? _____

2. Does the Andes mountain range go through Peru? _____

3. Through which country does most of the Amazon River flow?

_____

4. What country is just west of Suriname? _____

5. What four South American countries share Colombia's borders?

_____

6. In which country is Quito the capital city? _____

Death on Mount Everest

It was the **deadliest** day in Mount Everest's history. On May 10, 1996, a blizzard trapped 19 people near the summit. Among those stranded were Rob Hall and Scott Fischer, two of the best climbers in the world. But when a blizzard hits Nepal's Mount Everest, no one is safe. By the end of the storm, the lives of Hall, Fischer, and six other climbers were lost.

The Death Zone

Mount Everest is on the **border** between Nepal and China. In the spring of 1996, several groups were climbing Everest. They set up camps along the way.

On the 10th of May, 33 climbers were at Camp 4, 26,100 feet up the mountain. They only had to climb about 3,000 feet higher to reach the summit. At such heights, though, just breathing is hard work. Said one man, "Climbing above 26,000 feet, even with bottled oxygen, is like running on a **treadmill** and breathing through a straw."

In such thin air, a person's brain barely gets enough oxygen. So the person's thinking becomes confused. In addition, climbers often get headaches. They have trouble eating. They may lose their sight. They may even die. That is why anything above 26,000 feet is called "the Death **Zone**."

The climbers who headed for Mount Everest's summit on May 10 were at different skill levels. Some, like Hall and Fischer, were experts. Others were less experienced. Many had paid $65,000 each to be led up the mountain. Both Rob Hall and Scott Fischer were acting as guides for their groups.

An expert climber can reach the summit from Camp 4 in 12 hours. But on this day, it took longer. There was really only one trail the people could use. In places it was not very wide. Climbers had to go **single-file**. So when one person slowed down, everyone behind that person had to wait.

Seaborn Beck Weathers was among the climbers who tried for the summit that day. Soon, he began having eye trouble. At last, he decided to stop. He agreed to wait by the side of the trail while the others kept going. Rob Hall, his guide, promised to stop for him on the way back down. "Unfortunately, Rob never returned," Weathers later said.

A climber on Mount Everest

Killer Blizzard

While Weathers waited, Hall and Fischer led their **clients** up the mountain. Everyone had agreed to turn back at 2 P.M., no matter what. That way, they would be safe if a late afternoon storm blew in. But Hall and Fischer wanted to give people their money's worth. So both men ignored the 2 P.M. **deadline**.

After climbers reached the summit, they began to descend to Camp 4. But some people didn't reach the summit until after 3 P.M. Doug Hansen, one of Hall's clients, didn't get there until 4 P.M. Hall and Fischer waited for their slower clients. Then they also began to head down the mountain.

But a killer blizzard moved in late in the day. Suddenly, no one could see. The climbers became separated from each other. They ran out of bottled oxygen. A few lucky ones made it back to Camp 4. The rest were stuck in the high wind and driving snow in the Death Zone. "The storm was like a **hurricane**, maybe stronger," said one man.

The climbers headed to the peak, not knowing that a blizzard was about to hit.

Seaborn Beck Weathers tried to make it back to Camp 4 on his own. But he was too weak. As night settled over the mountain, Weathers just sank down into the deep snow and fell asleep.

Scott Fischer also gave up. At 27,200 feet, he simply stopped walking. Lobsang Jangbu, a Sherpa guide, was with him. Fischer told Lobsang to go on alone. But Lobsang did not want to do that. Finally, Fischer threatened to throw himself off the mountain. Only then did Lobsang leave his friend.

Rob Hall was stuck just below the summit. He was with his client Doug Hansen. Hansen had such bad **frostbite** that he couldn't walk. Hall would not leave him. He hoped that they could hang on until the storm let up. Then maybe help could reach them.

Mount Everest Wins

By morning, Scott Fischer was dead. So were Doug Hansen and five others. Rob Hall was still alive, but he was growing weaker by the minute. He talked with the people at the lower camps by radio. But with the storm still roaring, it was impossible to rescue him. Over the next few hours, Hall slowly froze to death.

Meanwhile, Seaborn Beck Weathers lay covered with ice. He had been unconscious most of the night. But suddenly he woke up. "Almost no one survives a night on Mount Everest, and I didn't expect to," he later said. Now he had to get moving or he really would die. Already his hands were frozen solid. Later, they would have to be cut off. His nose was black with frostbite. He would lose that, too. Weathers struggled to his feet and dragged himself down to Camp 4. His **arrival** was the one bit of happy news all day.

When people heard that eight climbers had died on Mount Everest, they were shocked. Those who knew the mountain were less surprised than most. Said one expert climber, "A human being does not belong on the summit of Mount Everest." Another said that when people try to fight mountains, "mountains will win every time."

Hall's team (left) and Fischer's team (right) posed for photos before the deadly climb.

Read and Remember — Check the Events

🔺 Place a check in front of the three sentences that tell what happened in the story.

_____ **1.** People paid money to be led up Mount Everest.

_____ **2.** No one was allowed to climb above the "Death Zone."

_____ **3.** Seaborn Beck Weathers twisted his ankle.

_____ **4.** A blizzard trapped many people near the summit.

_____ **5.** Doug Hansen carried Scott Fischer back to Camp 4.

_____ **6.** Rob Hall slowly froze to death.

Think About It — Find the Sequence

🔺 Number the sentences to show the correct order from the story. The first one is done for you.

_____ **1.** Several people died on Mount Everest.

__1__ **2.** On May 10, 1996, the climbers headed toward the summit.

_____ **3.** Seaborn Beck Weathers fell asleep in the deep snow.

_____ **4.** A killer blizzard moved in.

_____ **5.** Doug Hansen made it to the summit.

_____ **6.** The groups ignored the 2 P.M. deadline.

USE WHAT YOU KNOW

Focus on Vocabulary — Match Up

Match each word with its meaning. Write the correct letter in the blank.

_____ 1. deadliest

_____ 2. border

_____ 3. treadmill

_____ 4. zone

_____ 5. single-file

_____ 6. clients

_____ 7. deadline

_____ 8. hurricane

_____ 9. frostbite

_____ 10. arrival

a. storm with high winds and heavy rain

b. an area of land

c. most likely to kill

d. one at a time

e. time limit

f. the freezing of a part of a person's body

g. the act of getting to a place

h. the line that separates two countries

i. exercise machine for walking or running

j. people who pay for a service

Elevation

An area of land can have different **elevations**, or heights. Some areas have low plains. Other areas have tall mountains, such as the Himalayas. The map below uses colors to show different elevations in southern Asia. The map key shows which color is used for certain heights. Study the map and the map key. Circle the best answer to each question.

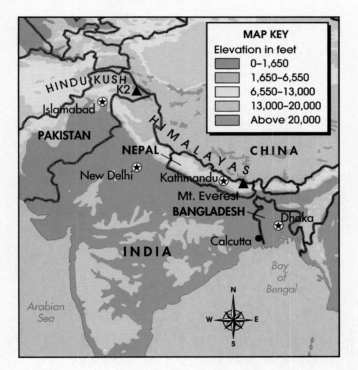

1. Which color shows the highest elevation?

   yellow   dark green   dark orange

2. What is the elevation of New Delhi?

   0–1,650 feet   1,650–6,550 feet   6,550–13,000 feet

3. In which part of India is the country's highest elevation?

   south   east   north

4. Which city has the lowest elevation?

   Calcutta   Kathmandu   Islamabad

Hanging by a
Thread

Deborah Lynn had never climbed a mountain before. Neither had her friends, Susan Hall and Nina Redman. It was a thrill for the three women to stand on the top of Washington's Mount Rainier. They had sweated and **strained** to the 14,411-foot peak. Now they were about to head back down. What they didn't know was that climbing up had been the easy part. The terrifying trip down would cost a fellow climber his life.

Avalanche!

Lynn and her friends had come to Mount Rainier as part of a group of 27 climbers. The group was led by **professional** guides. They began on June 10, 1998. By 10 A.M. the next day, they reached the top.

After staying there awhile, the group of climbers started back down. By 2:00 P.M. they were at 11,400 feet. There they came to an icy ridge between two large **glaciers**. Near it was a steep cliff. To be safe, the climbers roped themselves together in groups of five. Suddenly, someone yelled the one word that every mountain climber fears: "Avalanche!"

A huge wave of snow was sliding right toward Lynn and nine other climbers. The snow had been loosened by rising temperatures. Now it tumbled down the mountain, pulling with it everything in its path.

"We were told to run," Lynn later remembered. They had gone just a few steps when the avalanche hit them. Said Lynn, "I didn't even see or hear it."

Mount Rainier has many avalanches each year.

Lynn was tied to the same rope as Susan Hall. Both women went flying over the cliff. Luckily, the three other people on their rope did not go over the cliff's edge. As long as the rope held, Lynn and Hall would not fall to their death. But they were stuck, swinging in **midair**, staring at a 200-foot drop. A stream of icy water trickled down on Lynn. If she got cold enough, she would freeze to death.

Nina Redman was tied to a different rope. She and another climber, Patrick Nestler, were swept over the cliff, too. Nestler was tied to Redman's rope. He fell farther than any of the three women. He was also more seriously hurt. He hit some rocks as he fell. Cold water dripped on him as he swung in midair, just as it did on Deborah Lynn.

Rescue Efforts

Ruth Mahre

Back up on the ridge, the six other climbers didn't dare move. Ruth Mahre, one of the guides, said, "We were... **suspended** with our rope team hanging below us." They were lucky Mahre's rope had wrapped around a big rock and held tight. "If anybody moved, we were all going to go," Mahre added.

Climbers who were not caught in the avalanche hurried to the scene. They began putting up safety lines so they could pull Lynn and the others up onto solid ground. At the bottom of the mountain, other rescuers gathered. They piled into helicopters and tried to fly to the scene. But at 4,000 feet, thick fog blanketed the mountain. The pilots could not see where they were going. Until the fog lifted, there was nothing they could do.

A Long, Cold Wait

As the minutes passed, Lynn faced the fact that she might not get down the mountain alive. She later said, "One of the things I kept hearing was all the people above me shouting, 'Don't move!'... I guess the rope was **frayed** and close to breaking."

Lynn thought of her three children back home. She called out to Nina Redman, who also had small children. The two women made a deal. "We said if one of us doesn't make it, the other one has to tell her children how much she loved them," Lynn said.

Soon after that, Lynn slipped into a dream-like **state**. The icy water that dripped down on her was chilling her body. Lynn said, "I remember shivering and then I stopped shivering and just started turning **numb**." This meant that hypothermia was setting in. Lynn's body temperature was dropping too low.

Rescuers preparing to help the victims

Patrick Nestler faced the same danger. Shortly after the avalanche, he had called out to Redman. But since then, Nestler hadn't spoken a word. With icy water pouring over him, he was fighting hypothermia, too.

At last, rescuers got their safety lines set. They began the difficult job of pulling up the **stranded** climbers. First, they had to **rappel** down the cliff. That meant lowering themselves down the side of the cliff on ropes. They tied new ropes around each of the three women. Then they crawled back up the cliff to safety and began to pull. It took hours of careful work to bring Lynn, Hall, and Redman up.

At last, rescuers went down to get Patrick Nestler, who was the farthest away. "We were trying like crazy to get this last gentleman...," said one rescuer. But they were too late. By the time they got to Nestler, he had died from hypothermia.

Hall, Lynn, and Redman were loaded into rescue sleds, along with others who had been hurt in the avalanche. They were slowly moved down the trail toward the bottom of the mountain.

Just before dark, the fog around Mount Rainier broke. A helicopter flew in and picked up the injured climbers. They were rushed to a hospital.

Later, Deborah Lynn thanked those who had rescued her. She was happy to be home with her family. But, she added, "I don't think we'll be climbing any more mountains again soon."

The climbers who were not hurt by the avalanche headed down the mountain.

98

USE WHAT YOU KNOW

Read and Remember — Choose the Answer

▲ **Draw a circle around the correct answer.**

1. Where were the climbers when the avalanche hit them?

   at the base of Mount Rainier   at the summit   on a ridge

2. What kept the climbers from hitting the rocks below?

   rope   chains   snow

3. Who had water trickling down on them?

   Redman and Hall   Lynn and Nestler   Hall and Mahre

4. Which person died as a result of the avalanche?

   Nina Redman   Ruth Mahre   Patrick Nestler

5. What kept the helicopter from arriving sooner?

   fog   darkness   bright sunshine

Write About It

▲ **Imagine that you were Deborah Lynn. Write a letter to your family, describing what had happened on Mount Rainier and how you felt before the rescue.**

Dear _____,

_____

_____

_____

_____

_____

_____

_____

Focus on Vocabulary — Finish Up

▲ Choose the correct word in dark print to complete each sentence.

professional	**frayed**	**stranded**	**glaciers**
strained	**suspended**	**rappel**	**midair**
state	**numb**		

1. An object that is high above the ground is in _____.

2. Huge, slow-moving sheets of ice are called _____.

3. When a piece of rope is worn out or broken, it is _____.

4. To be stuck in a helpless position is to be _____.

5. If you have worked very hard to do something, you have _____ yourself.

6. The condition you are in is your _____.

7. To have no feeling in your body is to be _____.

8. A person who is an expert in a business is a _____.

9. To go down a cliff using a rope is to _____.

10. When you are hanging by a rope, you are _____ by it.

Route Map

A **route map** shows the roads and highways in an area. The map key shows the symbols used for different kinds of roads and highways. The route map below is of Washington. Study the map and the map key. Write the answer to each question.

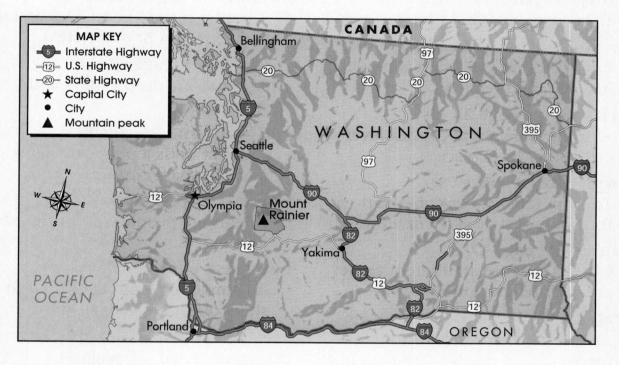

1. Which interstate highway would you take to get from Portland to Olympia? _____

2. Which interstate highway would you take to get from Seattle to Spokane? _____

3. What kind of highway crosses the north part of Washington? _____

4. Which two highways meet in Yakima? _____

5. Which U.S. highway is near Mount Rainier? _____

6. Which interstate highway is along the border between Washington and Oregon? _____

GLOSSARY

🌐 Words with this symbol can be found in the USE A MAP activities.

aboard   page 79
A person who is aboard an airplane is on that airplane.

agony   page 50
To be in agony is to be in great pain.

air current   page 39
An air current is air that is moving in a certain direction.

altitude   page 23
Altitude is height above sea level or another level place.

amputate   page 71
To amputate is to cut off a part of the body, such as a leg or a toe.

angles   page 47
Objects that are at different angles are in different positions.

arrival   page 90
An arrival is an act of getting to a place.

artificial   page 71
An object is artificial if it has been made by people instead of by nature.

ascend   page 8
To ascend means to climb up.

avalanche   page 47
An avalanche is a huge wall of snow sliding out of control.

blacksmith   page 15
A blacksmith makes horseshoes or other objects by heating iron and hammering it into shapes.

blizzard   page 9
A blizzard is a heavy snowstorm with strong winds.

border   pages 53, 85, 87
🌐 A border is the line that separates two countries or other areas.

canyons   page 17
Canyons are deep valleys with steep sides.

civilization   page 8
Civilization is a place where people live and share customs.

clients   page 88
Clients are people who pay experts for services.

compass   page 57
A compass is equipment used to show direction, such as north or south.

compass rose   page 21
🌐 A compass rose is a symbol on a map that shows direction.

confidence   page 49
Confidence is trust in one's abilities to do something.

conquered   page 24
Conquered means mastered or won. A climber who conquered a mountain was able to make the difficult climb to the top.

continent   page 13
🌐 A continent is a very large body of land, such as Africa.

crater　page 64
A crater is a hollow area in the ground or in a volcano.

crest　page 39
A crest is the top of a mountain.

crevasses　page 24
Crevasses are deep cracks in rock or in ice.

dangerously　page 58
Dangerously means in a way that is likely to cause harm.

deadliest　page 87
Deadliest means most likely to cause death.

deadline　page 88
A deadline is a time when a task should be finished.

death toll　page 65
A death toll is the number of people who lost their lives during an event such as a flood.

defeat　page 72
To defeat means to win a victory over.

degrees　pages 32, 37, 69
Degrees are units of measure for temperature or distance.

descend　page 41
To descend means to climb down.

desert　page 39
A desert is a dry area of land that has little rainfall and few plants.

desperate　page 18
When people are desperate, they have almost given up hope.

dismay　page 24
Dismay is a feeling of fear or alarm.

distance scale　pages 61, 77
A distance scale compares distance on a map with distance in the real world.

elevation　pages 55, 93
Elevation is height above a given level, such as sea level.

emergencies　page 57
Emergencies are sudden, serious events in which help is needed as soon as possible.

equator　pages 24, 29
The equator is an imaginary circle that runs east and west around Earth. It divides Earth equally into north and south.

eruption　page 63
An eruption is when something explodes or is released suddenly, such as gases or rocks from a volcano.

exhausted　page 42
Exhausted means very tired.

face　page 56
The face is the front or main surface, such as the face of a mountain.

failure　page 23
A failure is the act of not completing a goal or task.

fork　page 8
A fork is a place where a river divides.

frayed   page 97

Frayed means worn out. A frayed rope has strands that have become worn out or broken by rubbing.

frontier   page 15

A frontier is an area beyond the land where people have settled to live.

frostbite   page 89

Frostbite is the freezing of a part of a person's body, such as a hand.

glaciers   page 95

Glaciers are large sheets of ice and snow that move very slowly.

grief   page 80

Grief is a feeling of great sadness.

hemispheres   page 29

🌐 If the world is divided in half, it is divided into two hemispheres.

hometown   page 79

A hometown is the place where a person was born or grew up. It is also the place where a person lives.

hunch   page 81

A hunch is a guess or a feeling of knowing about something.

hurricane   page 88

A hurricane is a storm that has very strong winds and usually occurs with rain, thunder, and lightning.

hypothermia   page 56

Hypothermia is when a person's body temperature is very low. People in very cold air or water can be in danger of hypothermia.

ice axes   page 74

Ice axes are sharp tools used to chop or cut into ice.

incredible   page 82

Incredible means amazing or very hard to believe.

infection   page 17

An infection is a disease that is spread by a germ.

injuries   page 40

A person who has injuries is someone whose body has been hurt.

landmark   page 8

A landmark is a large object on land that is easy to see and helps people know where they are.

landscape   page 42

Landscape is the way an area of land looks.

latitude   pages 37, 69

🌐 Lines of latitude are imaginary lines that run east and west around Earth. They measure distance in degrees north and south of the equator.

ledge   page 39

A ledge is a rock that sticks out from the side of a mountain and looks like a narrow shelf.

longitude   pages 37, 69

🌐 Lines of longitude are imaginary lines that run north and south around Earth. They measure distance in degrees east and west of the 0° longitude.

map key   page 45

🌐 A map key tells what the symbols, colors, or patterns on a map mean.

mercy   page 66
To have mercy is to show pity or kindness.

metropolitan   page 79
A metropolitan area is a large, important city that has many people.

midair   page 96
An object in midair is one that is hanging or floating in air high above the ground.

mountaineering   page 71
Mountaineering is mountain climbing.

mountain range   page 8
A mountain range is a group of similar mountains that are close together.

Northern Hemisphere   page 72
The Northern Hemisphere is the part of Earth that is north of the equator.

numb   page 97
Numb means having no feeling. A person who is numb cannot feel heat, cold, or touch.

organization   page 66
An organization is a group of people who get together for a special purpose.

oxygen   page 74
Oxygen is a gas that is found in air. Animals and people need to breathe oxygen in order to live.

panic   page 33
Panic is a sudden and very powerful feeling of fear.

parachute   page 32
A parachute is a large piece of cloth that opens to catch wind and slow a person down.

pass   page 17
A pass is a low area in mountains, through which people can travel.

peaks   page 7
Peaks are the tops of mountains.

persisted   page 72
A person who persisted kept on trying to complete a difficult task.

physical disabilities   page 71
Persons with physical disabilities have a problem with a part of their body that limits their ability to do something, such as to see or walk.

plains   page 15
Plains are large areas of flat land.

plunge   page 24
To plunge is to fall suddenly.

porters   page 24
Porters are people who carry suitcases or equipment.

predict   page 63
To predict is to guess or tell what is going to happen before it occurs.

professional   page 95
A professional is a person who is an expert in a job or business.

progress   page 50
Progress is movement toward a goal.

rappel   page 97
To rappel means to go down a cliff by using a rope.

recovered   page 50

If something has been recovered, it has been found and brought back.

region   page 47

A region is an area of land.

reminder   page 48

A reminder is something that causes a person to remember.

remote   page 80

A remote place is one that is far away, is not easy to get to, or is hard to find.

representing   page 74

Representing means standing for, or serving as an example to others.

rescuers   page 57

Rescuers are people who help others who are hurt or are in dangerous places.

respect   page 34

To respect is to think well of or have regard for.

ridges   page 47

Ridges are long, narrow parts of mountains.

rim   page 64

A rim is the outer top edge of an object, such as a bowl, glass, or volcano.

risk   page 33

A risk is a possible danger or injury.

riverbed   page 42

A riverbed is ground over which a river flows or used to flow.

route map   page 101

A route map is a map that shows the roads and highways in an area.

sea level   page 31

Sea level is the average height of the surface of ocean water.

single-file   page 88

To walk in single-file means to walk one at a time.

slide   page 32

A slide is a group of rocks or dirt tumbling down a mountain or hill.

slope   page 31

A slope is ground that slants.

sources   page 7

Sources are the places where rivers begin.

Southern Hemisphere   page 79

The Southern Hemisphere is the part of Earth that is south of the equator.

state   page 97

A state is a person's condition. Being in a state describes how a person acts or feels.

strained   page 95

If a person strained to complete a task, she or he worked very hard.

stranded   page 97

A person is stranded if he or she is in a helpless position or is unable to get out of a place.

summit   page 7

A summit is the highest point on a mountain.

supported   page 23
When people have supported themselves, they have paid for their basic needs, such as food, clothing, and shelter.

survived   page 8
Survived means stayed alive.

survivors   page 80
Survivors are people who stay alive through a disaster, such as a flood or an airplane crash.

suspended   page 96
An object that is suspended is hanging in the air.

terrain   page 16
Terrain is the surface of the land. It is hard to travel on rough terrain.

tourists   page 63
Tourists are people who visit a place for pleasure or fun.

trading post   page 18
A trading post is a store for selling or trading goods.

tragedy   page 58
A tragedy is a very unhappy or terrible event.

treadmill   page 87
A treadmill is a machine on which a person exercises by walking or running in place.

triumph   page 26
A triumph is a victory or a great success.

ultimate   page 31
Ultimate means greatest or last.

unconscious   page 40
An unconscious person is one who is not awake.

unstable   page 47
Unstable means not steady or not firm.

utterly   page 34
Utterly means completely.

victims   page 66
Victims are people who were hurt or killed.

volcano   page 63
A volcano is a mountain or a hole in Earth's crust that can explode with lava, gases, hot rocks, or ashes.

volunteered   page 57
A person who volunteered to do something offered because he or she wanted to do it.

wagon train   page 18
A wagon train is a group of wagons that travel together over land.

wind-chill factor   page 56
Wind-chill factor is what the temperature feels like when the wind is blowing. It feels colder outside when it is windy.

wreckage   page 81
Wreckage is the broken pieces that are left after a crash.

zone   page 87
A zone is an area of land.

Did You Know?

◀ Do you think mountain climbers would like it on the moon? They probably would. Nearly all of the moon mountains are the height of Mount Everest, Earth's tallest peak!

◀ How high is 1,122 inches of snow? It's about as tall as a nine-story building. From 1971 to 1972, Mount Rainier in Washington received the most snowfall ever recorded in one year. About 1,122 inches of snow fell at the Rainier Paradise Ranger Station!

Could there really be a mountain ▶ taller than Mount Everest? Part of Mauna Kea, a mountain on an island of Hawaii, is hidden by the ocean. Mount Everest is the tallest mountain on land, but Mauna Kea is even taller. From its base on the bottom of the ocean to its peak, Mauna Kea is 33,476 feet high. That's 4,448 feet taller than Mount Everest!

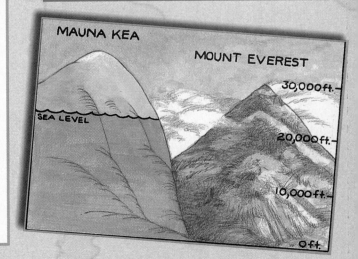

MAUNA KEA

MOUNT EVEREST

30,000 ft.

SEA LEVEL

20,000 ft.

10,000 ft.

0 ft.

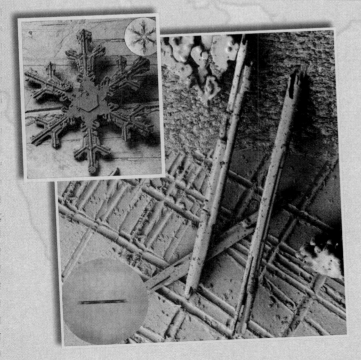

◄ Where could you pitch a tent if you were climbing up a steep mountain? On the side, of course. When mountain climbs last for many days, climbers must find a place to rest. Sometimes they hang a tent off the edge of the mountain. The tent hangs down the side of the steep cliff.

Did you know that mountains can ► grow? Sometimes layers of land below Earth's surface crash into each other. This causes the land on the surface to rise. Mount Everest grows more than an inch every year!

◄ Is it true that all snowflakes are alike? No two snowflakes are exactly alike. Most are six-sided star shapes. But some are not. When the air is very wet during a snowfall, tiny snow crystals are shaped like needles. These snow crystals stick together, causing the snowflakes to be long and thin like needles!

CHART YOUR SCORES

Score Your Work

1. Count the number of correct answers you have for each activity.
2. Write these numbers in the boxes in the chart.
3. Give yourself a score (maximum of 5 points) for **Write About It**.
4. Add up the numbers to get a final score for each tale.
5. Write your final score in the score box.
6. Compare your final score with the maximum score given for each story.

Tales	Read and Remember	Think About It	Write About It	Focus on Vocabulary	Use a Map	Score
Lost in the Mountains						/25
Mountain Man						/22
Queen of the Climbers						/23
To Ski the Tallest Mountain						/25
Nightmare in the Sierras						/24
A Climb to Remember						/26
A Killer Storm						/26
Volcano!						/22
Breaking the Record						/22
Against All Hope						/26
Death on Mount Everest						/23
Hanging by a Thread						/26

ANSWER KEY

Lost in the Mountains

Pages 6–13

Read and Remember — Finish the Sentence:
1. soldier 2. 1806 3. the cold 4. Pikes Peak
5. on foot

Think About It — Drawing Conclusions:
Answers will vary. Here are some possible
conclusions. 1. Thin clothes made it hard for the
men to stay warm in winter. 2. It is easier and faster
to travel on horses than on foot. 3. A blizzard made
it hard to find food. 4. Dougherty and Sparks could
not walk because their feet were frozen.

Focus on Vocabulary — Find the Meaning:
1. mountain tops 2. starting points 3. top
4. climb up 5. stayed alive 6. place where a river
divides 7. familiar object 8. cities and towns
9. group of mountains 10. bad snowstorm

Use a Map — Continents and Oceans:
1. seven 2. Africa, Europe, Asia, Australia,
Antarctica, North America, South America
3. Antarctica, Australia 4. Indian Ocean
5. Pacific Ocean 6. North America,
South America, Antarctica, Africa, Europe

Mountain Man

Pages 14–21

Read and Remember — Check the Events:
Sentences 2, 3, 5

Write About It: Answers will vary.

Focus on Vocabulary — Make a Word:
1. canyons 2. pass 3. plains 4. trading post
5. frontier 6. wagon train 7. desperate
8. infection 9. terrain 10. blacksmith
The letters in the circles spell *California.*

Use a Map — Map Directions:
1. east 2. Tampa 3. southwest 4. northwest

Queen of the Climbers

Pages 22–29

Read and Remember — Choose the Answer:
1. Matterhorn 2. money 3. guides and porters
4. six 5. a camera and film 6. Rudolph

Think About It — Find the Main Ideas:
Sentences 1, 5

Focus on Vocabulary — Crossword Puzzle:
ACROSS — 3. equator 5. plunge 7. conquered
9. altitude 10. porters; DOWN — 1. failure
2. triumph 4. supported 6. crevasses
8. dismay

Use a Map — Hemispheres:
1. Eastern Hemisphere 2. Western Hemisphere
3. Northern Hemisphere 4. Western Hemisphere
5. Eastern Hemisphere, Southern Hemisphere

To Ski the Tallest Mountain

Pages 30–37

Read and Remember — Finish the Sentence:
1. fast 2. the Himalayas 3. slow down 4. fell
5. death 6. hit a rock

Write About It: Answers will vary.

Focus on Vocabulary — Finish Up:
1. slope 2. degrees 3. panic 4. ultimate
5. slide 6. parachute 7. sea level 8. respect
9. risk 10. utterly

Use a Map — Latitude and Longitude:
1. 35°N 2. 105°W 3. Kilimanjaro
4. Mount Huascarán

Nightmare in the Sierras

Pages 38–45

Read and Remember — Check the Events:
Sentences 1, 4, 6

Think About It — Cause and Effect:
1. c 2. a 3. e 4. b 5. d

Focus on Vocabulary — Finish the Paragraphs:
1. desert 2. air current 3. crest 4. ledge
5. injuries 6. unconscious 7. descend
8. landscape 9. riverbed 10. exhausted

Use a Map — Map Keys:
1. ⌒ 2. no 3. small city 4. Sierra Nevada,
Coast Ranges 5. no 6. Owens River

A Climb to Remember

Pages 46–53

Read and Remember — Choose the Answer:
1. none 2. avalanches 3. more money 4. flags
5. by radio

Write About It: Answers will vary.

Focus on Vocabulary — Match Up:
1. c 2. f 3. a 4. d 5. i 6. b 7. g 8. j
9. h 10. e
Use a Map — Countries:
1. Kathmandu 2. India, China 3. India
4. India 5. Annapurna, Mount Everest 6. no

A Killer Storm

Pages 54–61
Read and Remember — Finish the Sentence:
1. blizzard moved in 2. snow cave 3. help 4. the weather improved 5. long poles 6. survived
Think About It — Fact or Opinion:
1. O 2. F 3. F 4. F 5. O 6. O
Focus on Vocabulary — Make a Word:
1. hypothermia 2. rescuers 3. volunteered
4. wind-chill 5. face 6. dangerously 7. compass
8. elevation 9. tragedy 10. emergencies.
The letters in the circles spell helicopter.
Use a Map — Distance Scale:
1. 3 inches 2. 300 miles 3. 150 miles 4. Spokane

Volcano!

Pages 62–69
Read and Remember — Check the Events:
Sentences 2, 5, 6
Write About It: Answers will vary.
Focus on Vocabulary — Crossword Puzzle:
ACROSS — 1. death toll 4. volcano 7. victims
8. rim 10. eruption; DOWN — 2. organization
3. tourists 5. crater 6. predict 9. mercy
Use a Map — Latitude and Longitude:
1. Guallatiri 2. Sangay 3. 14°N 4. Nevado del Ruiz

Breaking the Record

Pages 70–77
Read and Remember — Choose the Answer:
1. He got in shape. 2. Summit America
3. Denali 4. Adrian Crane's 5. high winds
6. a special artificial leg
Think About It — Find the Main Ideas:
Sentences 3, 6
Focus on Vocabulary — Finish the Paragraphs:
1. amputate 2. artificial 3. physical disabilities
4. mountaineering 5. Northern Hemisphere

6. oxygen 7. ice axes 8. defeat 9. persisted
10. representing
Use a Map — Distance Scale:
1. 2 inches 2. 600 miles 3. 300 miles 4. Nome

Against All Hope

Pages 78–85
Read and Remember — Finish the Sentence:
1. Andes 2. brother 3. thick bushes 4. look somewhere else 5. badly hurt
Write About It: Answers will vary.
Focus on Vocabulary — Find the Meaning:
1. place where someone grew up 2. lower half of the world 3. city 4. on the plane 5. people who stayed alive 6. far away 7. great sadness 8. guess
9. broken pieces from a crash 10. amazing
Use a Map — Countries:
1. La Paz 2. yes 3. Brazil 4. Guyana 5. Ecuador, Peru, Brazil, Venezuela 6. Ecuador

Death on Mount Everest

Pages 86–93
Read and Remember — Check the Events:
Sentences 1, 4, 6
Think About It — Find the Sequence: 6, 1, 5, 4, 3, 2
Focus on Vocabulary — Match Up:
1. c 2. h 3. i 4. b 5. d 6. j 7. e 8. a 9. f 10. g
Use a Map — Elevation:
1. dark orange 2. 0–1,650 feet 3. north 4. Calcutta

Hanging by a Thread

Pages 94–101
Read and Remember — Choose the Answer:
1. on a ridge 2. rope 3. Lynn and Nestler
4. Patrick Nestler 5. fog
Write About It: Answers will vary.
Focus on Vocabulary — Finish Up:
1. midair 2. glaciers 3. frayed 4. stranded
5. strained 6. state 7. numb 8. professional
9. rappel 10. suspended
Use a Map — Route Map:
1. Interstate Highway 5 2. Interstate Highway 90
3. state highway 4. Interstate Highway 82 and
U.S. Highway 12 5. U.S. Highway 12
6. Interstate Highway 84